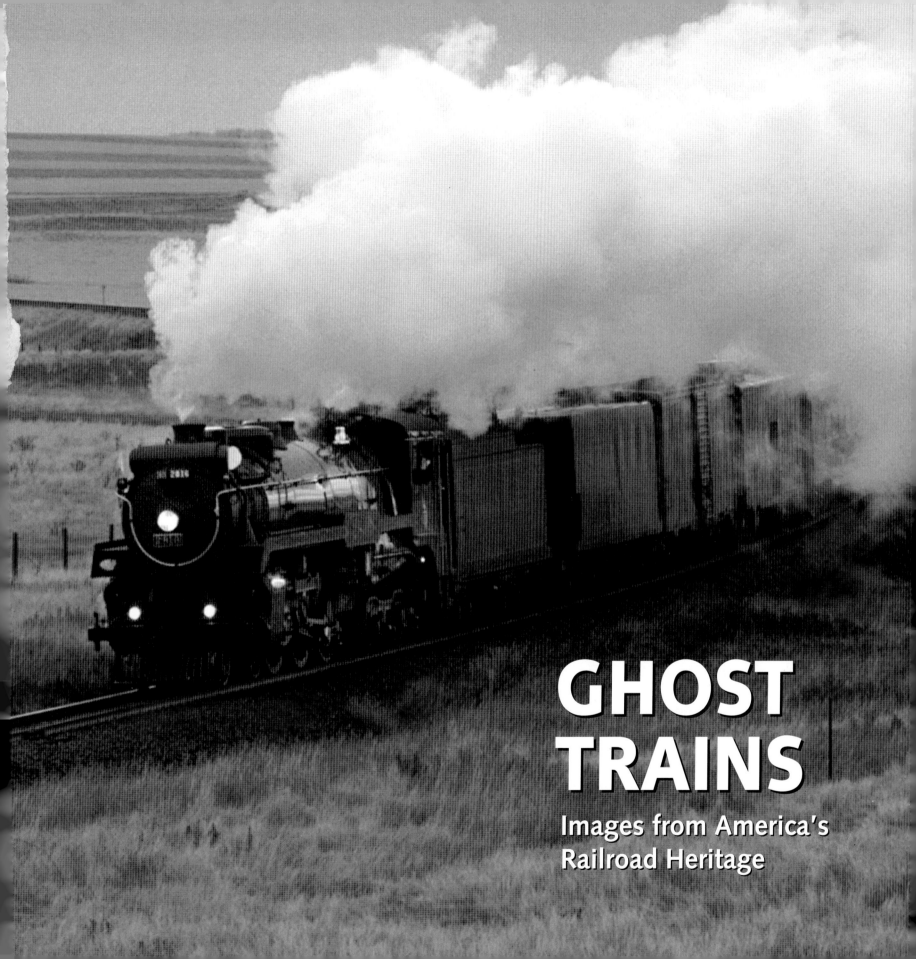

GHOST TRAINS

Images from America's
Railroad Heritage

UNION PACIFIC

844

GHOST TRAINS

Images from America's Railroad Heritage

James P. Bell

CHARTWELL
BOOKS, INC.

This edition published in 2014 by
CHARTWELL BOOKS, INC.
a division of BOOK SALES, INC.
276 Fifth Avenue Suite 206
New York, New York 10001
USA

Design and Repro by Philip Clucas MSIAD

ISBN-13: 978-0-7858-3083-2

Printed in China

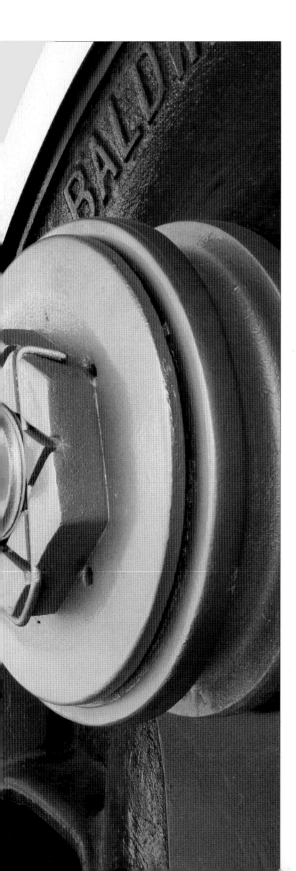

Contents

Introduction

What is it about trains that continues to fascinate people? My theory is that when the human genome is fully mapped, researchers are sure to isolate a DNA segment that identifies us as railfans and railroad photographers. It takes the activation of a genetic switch at a formative time in childhood to give a lifelong interest in trains.

This happened for me as a ten-year-old boy in 1958 when my family moved to northern California. My father was already there, starting his general contracting business and preparing a new home for our family. My mother, brother, and I traveled on Santa Fe's San Francisco Chief to join dad in the Bay Area. We journeyed from Arkansas to Kansas City on the Kansas City Southern Railway's Southern Belle and then headed west on the Santa Fe. I remember sitting long into the night in the dome car watching signals turn from green to red as we sped across the American Southwest. Eating meals in the diner formed vivid memories. Paintings of the red cliffs of New Mexico and Indian pueblos on the menus portrayed the same scenes passing by outside our dining car windows. From that time forward I was in love with western landscape and the trains that traveled through this spectacular country.

During the following years in the late 1950s and '60s I couldn't get enough of train watching. I remember Southern Pacific streamliners in the evenings winding past the C&H sugar refinery across the bay at Martinez in the evenings. Catching a glimpse of the California Zephyr gliding up the Feather River past our cabin formed lasting impressions on the emulsion of my young mind. At the public library I read about the world of railroading in the east and midwest, but I could only dream of visiting places like Horseshoe Curve or the speedways of Union Pacific across Nebraska and Wyoming until I became an adult. In those pre-internet days my favorite railroad books were by Charles Clegg and Lucius Beebe. Arthur Dubin's book, *Some Classic Train* expanded my universe. I saw great railroad photography in books by Dick Steinheimer, Jim Shaughnessy, and O. Winston Link.

For over 100 years railroads touched the lives of most Americans. For small town America, trains brought letters to our post office, picked up our milk and produce and took sons and daughters off to college, war, and new jobs. With the advent of interstate highways and air travel, railroads in the United States and Canada decreased in mileage and infrastructure after World War II. Depots, roundhouses, and other railroad structures disappeared rapidly. At times it seemed that what was left architecturally of the American railroad vanished at warp speed like the receding titles of a Star Wars movie. In the new millennium, abandoned right-of-ways and miles of seldom-used track remain. There is enough to remind us that trains once knitted us together as a country. A train of today rolling across the tracks of yesterday recalls the lives of our grandparents and great-grandparents from another era. We feel connected to the past by those steel rails across the landscape.

This collection of photo essays is an attempt in a way to capture and remember those ghost trains of the past and discover aspects of railroading and American history that we of a certain age only read about as young people. It is a great adventure to visit places of our childhood, sometimes remembered only from books, and try to imagine what it might have been like to pass through such a world on a train.

1 Roanoke, Virginia: A Railroad Town

Norfolk and Western steam locomotives No. 611 and No. 1218 simmered quietly in the railroad yard at the Virginia Museum of Transportation in Roanoke, Virginia in the gathering darkness of twilight. Smoke poured from their stacks and from around their steam cylinders. The aroma in the air resembled a mixture of backyard barbecue and 4th of July fireworks. A uniformed conductor checked his pocket watch, and "passengers" in vintage clothing boarded the night train. These days the two locos are normally on static display in an open-air train shed at the museum, but to recreate their glory days, they had been moved out onto open track for three days and nights of photography. The photographers dropped charcoal briquettes and kindling down the locos' smokestacks to produce realistic flames and billowing smoke. This trick brought the old engines back to life, visually at least. With both engines under steam, the atmosphere in the darkened siding was transported right back to 1955.

No. 611 is the last of the streamlined J-Class steam locomotives. The engine was built in 1950 by the Norfolk and Western Railway at a cost of $250,000. No. 611 ran at a steady 70mph and pulled coaches of up to 600 passengers between Norfolk, Virginia and all points west to Cincinnati, Ohio.

No. 611 entered service in May 1950. Just nine years later on October 24, 1959 this elegant bullet-nosed locomotive pulled her last revenue train, on a roundtrip via Roanake, Virginia and Bluefield, West Virginia. By then she had outlasted many other steam locos, which had already been consigned to overgrown sidings. Many steam engines became obsolete as many Americans took to the highways. No. 611 was lucky, along with No. 1218. Instead of being scrapped, both engines were retired to covered sidings at the Virginia Museum of Transportation in Roanake.

A northern type J-Class locomotive like No. 611 produces 5,200 horsepower, with a tractive effort of 80,000 pounds. This is delivered to the rails via a 70-inch diameter driving wheel. The engine weighs a total of 494,000 pounds.

LEFT: A volunteer at the Virginia Museum of Transportation plays the part of a railway worker at a special night photography session on July 12, 2013.

RIGHT: Norfolk and Western Railway steam locomotives Nos. 1218 and 611 are positioned for a special photo session at the Virginia Museum of Transportation on July 12, 2013.

After renovation at the museum, No. 611 was returned to active service in 1981 as part of the railroad's steam program. The engine was used for special excursions, along with engine No. 1281, until the early 1990s. The Voyageur Press title *Steam Trains*, records both locos in full steam during one of these excursions. Only fourteen J-class engines were ever built and No. 611 is now the only one in existence.

No. 1218 was built in 1943 in just over two weeks. This was at a time when strong and reliable locomotives were needed to assist the war effort. This amazing two week construction time was a record at the Norfolk & Western's Birmingham, Alabama workshops. Back then, the engine cost $163,872. No. 1218 hauled troops and equipment for the military as well as coal. An A-class engine like No. 1218 could pull either 190 fully-loaded coal cars (weighing 170,000 tons) between Williamson, West Virginia and Portsmouth, Ohio, or 200 passenger cars (weighing 180,000 tons) between Crewe and Norfolk, West Virginia. Like No. 611, No. 1218 had a 70-inch driving wheel, but had a much greater tractive effort of 114,000 pounds, and a gross weight of 573,000 pounds.

No. 1218 began service on June 2, 1943 and regularly pulled coal trains on the 252 mile journey between Roanoke, Virginia and Norfolk, Virginia. The engine ran at a top speed of 70mph and pulled its last train in July 1959. Ignominiously, No. 1218 was sold with two of its classmates to Union Carbide. The engines were destined to serve as stationary boilers. Luckily, No. 1218 survived virtually intact. In 1963, the engine was purchased by Nelson Blount as a steam locomotive exhibit for his Steamtown collection at Bellow's Falls, Vermont. Six years later, No. 1218 was

RIGHT: Peter Lerro places charcoal into the stack of N&W steam locomotive No. 1218 to produce smoke effects for a special photo shoot at the Virginia Museum of Transportation on July 13, 2013.

ABOVE: A volunteer at the Virginia Museum of Transportation is dressed as a conductor handing up orders to a passing steam locomotive, N&W No. 1218. The image is all simulation as the locomotive is not under steam on a special photo shoot on July 13, 2013 in Roanoke, Virginia.

RIGHT: Volunteers in 1940s era costume board a N&W passenger coach during a special photo shoot in Roanoke, Virginia on July 13, 2013.

acquired by the Virginia Museum of Transportation and put on static display at the museum. It was not until 1985 that the engine was sent back to the Birmingham workshop where it was first made to be fully renovated. After two years of painstaking work, the A-class locomotive finally returned to full steam in 1987. No. 1218 and No. 611 pulled regular steam excursions until the early 1990s.

Photographers sometimes do night photo sessions in Roanoke using the museum's vintage locomotives. They probably draw some inspiration from another rail photographer, the legendary O. Winston Link. Link documented the last days of steam trains along the N&W in the mid-1950s. Locomotives No. 611 and No. 1218 even appeared in some of his images.

The drama of the N&W in the Blue Ridge Mountains intrigued Link. Over a period of several years he drove from his commercial studio in New York City and photographed the N&W at night using multiple banks of flashbulbs to light the passing trains for his Speed Graphic cameras. He photographed not only the trains, but the people, homes, and country stores along the line, all with passing trains in the background. Link left a lasting legacy of life in the Blue Ridge. He even took movie footage and recorded the lonesome sounds of steam engines in the mountains.

LEFT: Actors in costume pose on the platform of the Virginia Museum of Transportation as N&W No. 611 appears to approach under steam on July 13, 2013.

RIGHT: N&W No. 611 and a vintage automobile are positioned in the same frame in this photo session at the Virginia Museum of Transport-ation in Roanoke on July 13, 2013.

RIGHT: Steps lead to the Roanoke Hotel in Roanoke, Virginia. Across the street from the hotel is the former N&W Railway depot that is now the O. Winston Link Museum.

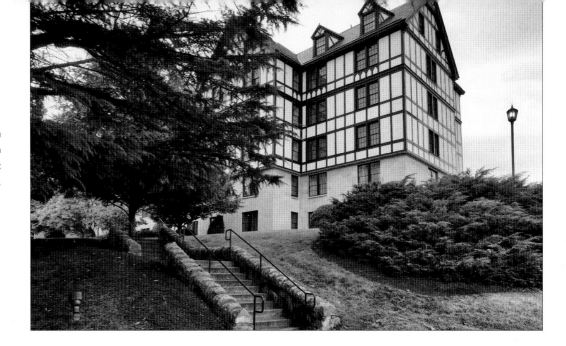

BELOW: The former N&W Railway depot is now the entrance to a visitor center and the O. Winston Link Museum in Roanoke, Virginia.

A museum named for Link is today located in the former N&W depot, an Art Moderne structure that sits down the green, grassy hill from the Roanoke Hotel. The depot, the hotel, and nearby Art Deco office buildings were all built by the N&W Railway in the early to mid-1900s. The Roanoke Hotel, different in design from the N&W depot and office buildings, is a classic inn built in the 1882 Tudor style. The hotel sits on a hill over the city and grew through additions and renovations over the years. After 107 years of operation, the hotel closed its doors in 1989. The Norfolk Southern, successor to the N&W, donated the complex to the Virginia Tech Real Estate Foundation. With restoration funds from the city of Roanoke and the Foundation, the hotel reopened and became a key part in the reinvigorated downtown Roanoke.

Some of the photography group stayed at the hotel. A room facing the tracks is always a prime spot. The Virginia Museum of Transportation is only a short two-block walk from the hotel: an enclosed glass pedestrian bridge takes guests over the Norfolk Southern mainline to downtown Roanoke.

The N&W No. 611 last ran in 1994 before its return to the museum where she has sat on display. The museum has organized a committee investigating the feasibility of restoring No. 611 to mainline excursion service. "Fire Up 611" is the campaign soliciting donations for the project. Someday the smoke and steam over Roanoke may be real, not just the simulation of smoke by charcoal briquettes, as ghosts of the Powhatan Arrow and Pocahontas return to the Blue Ridge when N&W 611 steams again.

ABOVE: N&W No. 1218 and N&W No. 611 appear to be under steam at the Virginia Museum of Transportation in this simulation for a photo session in Roanoke, Virginia on July 13, 2013.

BELOW: Pete Lerro holds a box of TNT Ammo Smoke used in his simulations of locomotives under steam for a special night photo session on July 13, 2013 at the Virginia Museum of Transportation.

2 The TAT and Waynoka: For a Brief Shining Moment

In 1991 I was flying my vintage Piper Cherokee over Waynoka, Oklahoma when my buddy and I spotted the former Santa Fe Harvey House and depot situated on the southern transcontinental line of the Santa Fe Railroad from F City to Albuquerque, New Mexico. A few miles from town we saw the old airfield chosen personally by Charles Lindbergh in 1928. This airport was now just a cow pasture with an abandoned concrete apron bordered by all that remained of two brick service buildings and a modern day barn. It was hard to believe that 65 years before, Waynoka (population 937 in 1992) was an important junction on the national route of the Transcontinental Air Transport. I had to turn my Cherokee west toward the present day Waynoka Municipal Airport in order to land.

Sandie Olsen, director of the Waynoka Historical Society, met us at the small airport and drove us into town to tour the Santa Fe depot and former Harvey House. Olson was eager to tell us about her town and the important role the community played in history.

Imagine 1928. The Roaring Twenties were in full stride. Charles Lindbergh had just crossed the Atlantic solo in the Spirit of St. Louis. Most Americans still traveled by train, but fledgling airlines were coming into existence and creating competition for rail travel. There was only one problem: airplanes didn't have adequate navigation radios yet to travel at night, and airfields were not well lighted. A train trip across the country took 4 days of travel. The Transcontinental Air Transport, lead by Clement Key of the Curtis Airplane Company, planned to change that equation by shortening the usual four day travel time to just two days using a combination of air and rail conveyances. Charles Lindbergh was part of this company, and with his flying skills he personally picked the towns and airfield sites along the way for this cooperative system.

LEFT: A Santa Fe Railroad diesel locomotive pulls into the historic Santa Fe depot in Waynoka, Oklahoma in late 1991.

RIGHT: A Santa Fe Railroad freight train waits for a crew change at the historic Santa Fe depot and former Harvey House in Waynoka, Oklahoma in late 1991.

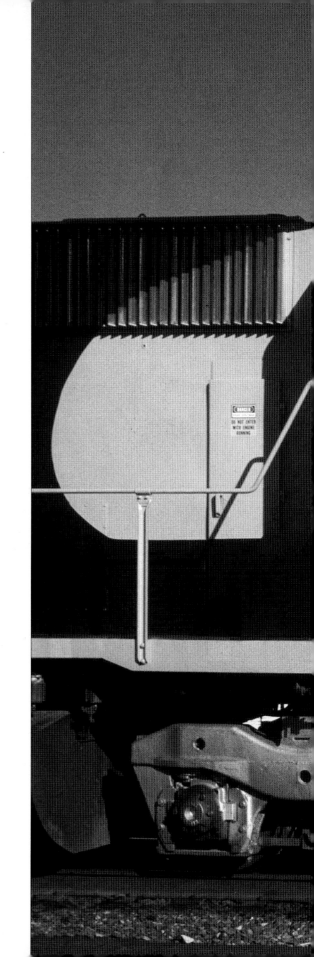

Construction on the TAT airport in Waynoka began on March 3, 1929. When completed, the airfield boasted the country's third largest hanger in the country. The runway was lighted and there was also an airport beacon light.

The inaugural trip on the TAT started in New York City on July 7, 1929. On the other side of the nation in ceremonies in Glendale, California's TAT facility, Grand Central Air Terminal, Charles Lindbergh pushed a button that activated a flashing light in Grand Central Station in New York City where a crowd had gathered to celebrate the air-rail service inauguration. At that point Pennsylvania Railroad's overnight train, the Airline Express, bound for Columbus, Ohio departed from New York. These record-breaking travelers awoke on July 8, at Port Columbus where they boarded two Ford Tri-Motor aluminum aircraft for the flight across the middle of the country to Waynoka. That morning on July 8 in Glendale, Lindbergh personally piloted the first eastbound Ford Tri-Motor, the City of Philadelphia, eastbound bound for Waynoka with the first stop in Winslow, Arizona.

BELOW: A Ford Trimotor is on approach to Jones Airport in Tulsa, Oklahoma on September 15, 2007. The vintage airplane is base at the EAA AirVenture Museum in Oshkosh, Wisconsin and is on tour giving rides throughout the Midwest.

ABOVE: A map at the Air-Rail Museum in the former Harvey House and Santa Fe Railroad depot in Waynoka, Oklahoma shows the route of the Transcontinental Air Transport in 1929. The route shortened travel across the United States from four days to two days by a combination of air and rail travel. The TAT later became TWA.

The westbound air passengers arriving in Waynoka came from the TAT airfield to the railroad station in a specially designed streamlined trailer called an Aero Car pulled by a Packard automobile. They enjoyed dinner in the Fred Harvey Restaurant at the Harvey House in the depot and boarded a Santa Fe night train that arrived the next morning in Clovis, New Mexico. Once more the adventurous travelers flew Ford Tri-Motors to Glendale's TAT terminal during the daytime. Those first passengers flying west of Clovis and east of Glendale during daylight hours got a good look at the grandeur of the American Southwest from the air. Months later, Mrs. Eugene Batten said of her flight on the TAT, "To you I owe one of the greatest and most joyful events of my life-the perfect trip. Surely crossing the desert via TAT is the ideal way."

ABOVE: The former Santa Fe depot and Harvey House restaurant in Waynoka, Oklahoma now houses an Air-Rail Museum and a Mexican restaurant. The rail line now belongs to the Burlington Northern Santa Fe Railroad.

LEFT: In Manhattan, Kansas on September 2007 a 1929 Ford Trimotor, NC8407, is inspected by a volunteer pilot flying the aircraft from Tulsa, Oklahoma to Lincoln, Nebraska.

ABOVE: The dual controls on Ford Trimotor, NC84017, give ample area for the pilot to handle the aircraft in flight.

The 48-hour travel time between the coasts was a hit. The TAT flew 500,000 miles and carried almost 3,000 passengers in the company's first 6 months of existence. In-flight movies were offered with feature films, newsreels, and cartoons. Fred Harvey Company, the Santa Fe hotel and dinning car company, developed special tablecloths, china, and meals for the TAT service. The TAT proved popular with the Hollywood set traveling between New York and California.

At the Waynoka depot and Harvey House on in 1991, I met Helen Chapman, aged 80, one of Olson's friends with a connection to the Santa Fe Railroad and the TAT: she had been a Harvey Girl in Waynoka. Harvey Girls were the young women who served meals and worked in Fred Harvey hotels and dining rooms. These women lived in college-like dormitories and Harvey service offered a way for these young women to enter the work force and gain some degree of independence. Chapman recalled the exciting days of the TAT and her time as a Harvey Girl. Celebrities such as Amelia Earhart, the Lindberghs, Will Rogers, and Myrna Loy came across the Waynoka depot platform.

On September 3, 1929, a TAT Ford Tri-motor crashed into Mt. Taylor, New Mexico west of Albuquerque. All people on board perished in one of the first commercial airline crashes in the U.S. The stock market then crashed on Black Friday, October 29, 1929. This caused more problems for the TAT. Airplanes began flying at night with better radio navigation and airport lighting systems. After all of the companies' planning, success and improvement, it was surely disappointing to the investors, patrons, and Waynoka residents that the TAT only lasted for 16 months. The airline later became Trans World Airlines. The TAT air-rail venture melted into history. Waynoka returned to its slumber on the high plains of western Oklahoma. In 1939, the great hanger at the TAT airport in Waynoka was sold and moved to Little Rock, Arkansas where it still serves today for Central Flying Service.

After I flew home back to Arkansas in 1991, it would be 2010 before I returned to Waynoka. During my second visit, Sandie Olson again showed me around the Waynoka Harvey House and Santa Fe depot. She was in the process of organizing the new Air-Rail Museum that told the story of Waynoka and the TAT. The railroad was now the Burlington Northern Santa Fe. Helen Chapman had passed away taking with her the many stories of her Fred Harvey Days. But there was now a restaurant in the old Harvey House, a Tex-Mex restaurant serving good food.

As Olson showed me around the new museum in the depot complex, I told her about the trip I had just completed. I had flown from Tulsa, Oklahoma to Lincoln, Nebraska on a Ford Tri-Motor from the AirVenture Museum in Oshkosh, Wisconsin. The plane had been down in Oklahoma giving rides at Tulsa's Jones Airport. The Ford Tri-Motor was flying a deadhead move from Tulsa to Lincoln, Nebraska for the next weekend of rides. The volunteer pilot, a Northwest Airlines commercial pilot, who enjoyed flying an airliner from the 1920s said, "Yes," when I asked him if I could ride along as a passenger. I didn't care that I would have to rent a car and drive back one way from Lincoln to Tulsa when the trip was finished. It is not every day you get to ride in a Tri-Motor as a passenger.

We landed once in Manhattan, Kansas to refuel and then made the final leg to Lincoln. I rented a car to drive back to Tulsa, stopping in Waynoka on my way. I now knew what it felt like to fly a Tri-Motor low and slow over the heart of the Great Plains. How right it felt to visit again this small Oklahoma town that for a brief shining moment had the world's attention as a railroad and airline interchange on the Transcontinental Air Transport.

ABOVE: The Ford Trimotor from the EAA AirVenture Museum in Oshkosh, Wisconsin is in Tulsa, Oklahoma at Jones Airport on September 17, 2007. The plane is being prepared for a flight to Lincoln, Nebraska as part of the museum's Midwest tour.

LEFT: The metal logo of the Ford Motor company in Dearborn, Michigan is riveted to the tail of Trimotor NC8407. The plane is in Tulsa, Oklahoma on September 17, 2007.

RIGHT: A Burlington Northern Santa Fe freight train passes close to the remnants of the 1929 TAT airport outside of Waynoka, Oklahoma on September 18, 2007. The buildings and a concrete pad are all remains of this historic airfield.

3 *True Grit,* Remake of a Classic

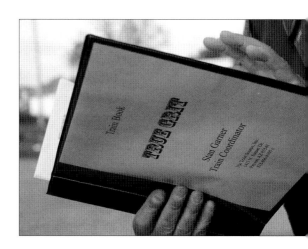

When the Coen Brothers planned the remake of the original John Wayne movie *True Grit* they chose to make it in Granger, Texas rather than Fort Smith, Arkansas where the historical action had actually taken place. However a piece of Arkansas's steam heritage, the Reader Railroad's No. 2 locomotive, did star in the film.

No. 2 was built by the Baldwin Locomotive works in January 1907, but the locomotive looks much older. No. 2's design owes more to the nineteenth century than the twentieth, which meant that the engine fitted perfectly into a movie about the Old West. The Baldwin Locomotive Works was originally located in Philadelphia, Pennsylvania. Later, it was re-located to nearby Eddystone, Pennsylvania. As steam

LEFT: Stan Garner, reviews his script before the day's filming of train sequences for *True Grit* on April 29, 2010 in Granger, Texas.

RIGHT: Production crew and Reader Railroad fireman, Steven Greathouse, apply temporary paint and weathering to steam locomotive No. 2.

BELOW: Actors driving horses and wagons and the Reader Railroad steam train crew prepare for the next scene during the filming of Paramount Pictures' *True Grit* in Granger, Texas on April 29, 2010.

LEFT: Production staff and film crew for the movie, *True Grit*, prepare a stack of railroad ties on the track for a scene recreating old Fort Smith, Arkansas. The location for the movie making is Granger, Texas.

ABOVE: Background extras in period costume wait for direction in a scene recreating old Fort Smith, Arkansas for the filming of Paramount Picture's *True Grit* in Granger, Texas on April 29, 2010.

declined, Baldwin stopped producing locomotives in 1956 and went out of business completely in 1972.

No. 2 was built for the Lufkin Land & Lumber Company that built the Texas and Louisiana Railroad. In 1902, the company built twenty-two miles of track between Lufkin and Monterey to gain access to the timber it owned. As the timber along the track became depleted, the line was abandoned in the 1930s. Lufkin sold its locomotives, including No. 2.

No. 2 went on to serve the Shreveport, Houston & Gulf Railroad, the Carter-Kelley Lumber Company, the W.T. Carter and Brother Lumber Company, the Scott & Bearskin Lake Railroad, and (finally) Richard Grigsby's Reader Railroad. At the invitation of Paramount's train coordinator for the film, Stan Garner, Grigsby and his team joined the movie crew in Granger, Texas, on April 28, 2010.

Garner lives in Payson, Arizona. Grigsby and Garner had previously worked together in other western movies like *3:10 to Yuma* and *There Will Be Blood* using the Reader Railroad movie train. Grigsby's railroad or his steam trains have appeared in other films like *Appaloosa, Boxcar Bertha* and *O' Brother Where Art Thou*. Garner has supervised or acted in 15 movies and television productions involving trains and railroads, and he has appeared on camera as a train conductor in movies such as *Iron Will, The Adventures of Young Indiana Jones,* and *Under Siege, Dark Territory.*

Granger is a small town about an hour north of the Texas capitol in Austin. The thriving movie industry in Austin supplied the ancillary personnel and support crews needed for a major motion picture like *True Grit*. The production crew did a great job in making tiny Granger look like 1880s Fort Smith. False fronts dressed up many of the buildings and wooden sidewalks. Dirt on the streets and smoke from charcoal

LEFT: Richard Grigsby, owner of the Reader Railroad movie train from Arkansas, smiles as the last shots of a day's filming occurs on the movie set of *True Grit* in Granger, Texas on April 29, 2010.

RIGHT: The movie train from Reader, Arkansas is placed onto a siding after a day of filming in the Paramount Picture's remake of *True Grit* in Granger, Texas on April 29, 2010.

fires completed the picture adding authenticity for the cameras. When all of the extras and the horses with wagons took their places, a scene emerged resembling the museum's historical photographs I had seen of my hometown's frontier years. The art department of the movie production relied upon those same historic photographs in converting Granger into old Fort Smith.

Using a similar method as in *Appaloosa, 3:10 to Yuma*, and *There Will Be Blood*, Grisgby transported his movie train from Reader, Arkansas to the location in Texas by using trucks and the highways. Grigsby loaded Reader steam locomotive No. 2 onto a lowboy trailer and pulled the load to Granger by tractor truck. Similarly, heavy duty truck wheels were placed under each coach for transport. These rigs were equipped with mud flaps on the rear, and each individual coach was pulled by its own tractor truck over the highway to Granger.

"Hello, I'm from the real Fort Smith," became my greeting when I met new people on the movie set. As the photographer for the Reader Railroad and Grigsby, my job was to document the use of the steam train from Arkansas in this classic movie about Arkansas. The extras, horse wranglers, and myriad of other support people in the production seemed to enjoy their part in recreating the old West.

The entire town of Granger gave itself over to the film for several weeks. Since a film crew often works on its stomach, the school cafeteria was commandeered as the main eating area. Catering trucks tucked away on the side streets of the movie set provided drinks and snacks in between meals. A highlight for the steam engine crew was meeting an Arkansas actor, Roy Jones, Sr., who played the part of Varnell in the film. Varnell is the African-American farm hand who accompanies young Mattie Ross from her farm in Yell County, Arkansas to Fort Smith. There she plans to find the murderer of her father.

Roy Lee Jones, Sr. came into the dining hall soon after he arrived in Granger. He sat down with the steam crew and told us his story. He is a movie and television actor from, Humphrey, Arkansas. He now lives in Los Angeles, California. Jones told us of his acting career and life as a jazz musician. He flew into Texas just for two days of filming and appears in the opening scenes when he and Mattie Ross get off the train in Fort Smith.

On April 28, 2010, the Arkansas crew readied steam locomotive No. 2 for its cameo roll in the movie. Just as the engine was about to be steamed up, the crew discovered that an important piece of equipment on the locomotive had been damaged in transit to Granger. One of the two pop-off safety valves had been bent. The locomotive required both these valves to operate safely. A scramble began to find another pop-off valve. Part of the Arkansas team drove back to Reader, Arkansas to bring back a second safety valve. Grigsby also ordered another safety valve that came by special courier from the Houston area. Both safety vales arrived on the evening of the 28th and the crew worked late into the night ensuring the locomotive's readiness for filming the next morning.

Reader No. 2 performed flawlessly during the day on filming on April 29. The presence of a steam train on the set energized the movie cast and crew. How appropriate that a small piece of Arkansas had a role in this major motion picture about Arkansas. When I first saw this new film in the theater in December 2010, I felt the Coen brothers had surpassed the first *True Grit*. With a musical score utilizing Christian hymns and the movie's theme of devotion to friends and family, this movie seemed like a song to my hometown.

4 The Tuskegee Airmen

As long as Hollywood makes movies about stateside life during World War II , they'll need passenger trains and railroad depots. Don Ball's book title from several years ago said it all: the 1940's was indeed "the decade of trains." On February 25, 1995, film makers returned to the Arkansas and Missouri Railroad and Fort Smith in northwestern Arkansas for a segment of another wartime movie, *The Tuskegee Airmen*.

This film tells the story of a squadron of black airmen in 1942 who faced the hazards of flying combat aircraft and persevered against prejudice in the days of "Whites Only" drinking fountains and segregated transportation. Red Tails, Inc. produced this film for HBO. The company's name referred to the tail sections of aircraft painted red as an insignia of the black squadron. Directed by Robert Markowitz, the film starred Laurence Fishburne, Cuba Gooding, Jr, and Malcolm Jamal Warner.

Much of the movie's action involved vintage World War II aircraft, especially P-51 Mustangs, flying simulated combat missions at Muskogee Oklahoma's Davis Field. A large number of the barracks and classrooms scenes utilized Fort Chaffee, a U. S. Army training post near Fort Smith, Arkansas.

In one poignant scene in the movie, the principal characters were thrown off the white section of a southern train in Hillsboro, Alabama. The black recruits had to decide whether to return the train and ride in the "Jim Crow" coach or forget about becoming pilots and go home. They return to the train in the "colored" section, but watched in anger as German prisoners of war were given the "white" seats they have just vacated.

To film this sequence, the Arkansas and Missouri Railroad brought their passenger train to Fort Smith from the line's headquarters in Springdale, Arkansas. The four-car passenger train consisted of an 1899 Boston and Maine combine and three heavyweight steel coaches, the Biloxi Blues, Golden Age, and

LEFT: A technician directs a spotlight for the filming of train scenes in the HBO movie, *The Tuskegee Airmen*, in Fort Smith, Arkansas on February 25, 2010. The movie used vintage automobiles and the former Frisco Station in Fort Smith.

Mountain View. Attached to the end of a southbound freight on February 24, the passenger train was dropped off in Fort Smith yard in preparation for the next day's filming. I planned to photograph the railroad's part in the movie.

An Alco T-6 diesel locomotive coupled on to the passenger train and backed the half-mile from the A&M yard into Fort Smith's former Frisco station. Location scout Paul Marcus of Chicago seemed pleased to have found the concrete and granite depot in such good condition. A large "Buy Defense Bonds" billboard painted by a local artist, Ralph Irwin, combined with vintage automobiles gave a solid 1940s feel to the set. An upscale Mexican restaurant operated from the renovated station facility.

"We liked the feel of this depot," Marcus said. "It had a substantial presence to it. We had considered the Van Buren depot for awhile, but it seemed too cute, too Victorian." Van Buren, across the Arkansas River, also has a restored Frisco depot on the A&M mainline. In 1987 Van Buren and the A&M appeared in *Biloxi Blues*, another WWII motion picture.

RIGHT: Background extras wait for their call to the next scene during filming of *The Tuskegee Airmen* at the former Frisco Station in Fort Smith, Arkansas on February 25, 2013.

FAR RIGHT: Jim Fields is an actor from Dallas, Texas who portrayed the train conductor in the HBO, *The Tuskegee Airmen*, in Fort Smith, Arkansas.

ABOVE: Rehearsal of a scene from *The Tuskegee Airmen* occurs on the platform of Frisco Station in Fort Smith, Arkansas on February 25, 1995.

LEFT: Vintage vehicles and the Arkansas and Missouri Railroad passenger train are in place as actors wait for the next scene for the HBO film, *The Tuskegee Airmen*.

The whole movie set was evocatively lit, as most of the outdoor action would take place at night. Some filming inside the coaches had already taken place during the day, to take advantage of the daylight. Several period vehicles were parked outside the old Frisco Train Depot at the Fort Smith National Historic Site to complete the authentic feel of a wartime train station. A Willys jeep, a familiar sight in the war years, is parked in the foreground. In the middle distance of the photograph, a young couple stand behind their aero-style coupe, which dates from the late 1930s. The wet pavements reflect the eerie lighting, completing the atmosphere of a humid Southern night.

As I watched, workers sprayed the pavement with a fire hose to simulate a rainy southern evening. Drivers parked antique cars near the tracks. High-intensity floodlights on the roof of the depot illuminated the passenger train and depot platform.

Police halted traffic on nearby roads as the Panavision lenses were focused and sound equipment was readied. Smoke generating machines provided the atmospheric look of steam and coal smoke along the depot platform.

"Silence," director Markowitz barked. "Action," and the cameras rolled.

"Either get on or back away," demanded movie railroad conductor Jim Fields. Glaring at the black recruits, he shouted, "All aboard."

Fishburne, Walker, and Gooding ran through their paces of returning to the train several times before Markowitz was satisfied. Filming carried over into the early morning hours with numerous retakes of scenes from different angles.

It takes a wide range of people to make a movie come together. Production assistants attended to details. A still photographer hooked Polaroids around his neck on a beaded chain for reference to costume details later. The owner of the antique cars repositioned his vehicles. Extras stood or sat on suitcases in their places waiting for direction in their background movements. A paramedic who left her ambulance job to work on this movie, tended to any aches and pains of the cast and crew. Catered food from the Mexican restaurant in the Frisco station revived everyone.

At 1:30 a.m. the assistant director said that filming was done. Actors scurried for their private dressing trailers. The extras exchanged the movie company's vintage clothing and props for their Reeboks and backpacks. New friends said their goodbyes as crews took down the spotlights and hidden electrical cords. With two whistle blasts, the A&M passenger train eased back down to the local yard to await return to Springdale. The movie magic of the evening was slowly dissipating.

The illusions of Hollywood are fleeting, but for that short time on a Saturday evening, million dollar lighting and a cast of characters with a train gave us a glimpse of what Fort Smith's old Frisco station might have looked like 50 years ago.

LEFT: Waiting for the call to their next scene, extras rest on their luggage during filming.

RIGHT: Laurence Fishburne, left, and Jim Fields, right, have finished a night of filming on the set of *The Tuskegee Airmen* in Fort Smith, Arkansas at the Frisco Station train platform. Fishburne starred in the HBO movie and Fields portrayed the train conductor.

5 *Appaloosa* on the Old Santa Fe

When Richard Grigsby received the call to provide equipment for movie train sequences in the western film, *Appaloosa*, in Santa Fe, New Mexico, Grigsby did not move the train over the railroads. He resorted to the highways. His steam crew gathered at Reader, Arkansas late in September 2007. They winched Reader No. 2, a 37-ton locomotive, onto a trailer and placed the tender onto a second trailer. Rubber tires and mud flaps were bolted under each of the boxcars and the two wooden coaches that comprised the movie train train. The crew then hauled the five loads over the highways from Arkansas into Texas and on to northern New Mexico. They used tractor trucks for each individual rig.

At Lamy, New Mexico, Grigsby directed placement of the train onto the tracks of the Santa Fe Southern Railway. Lamy is a picturesque adobe village at the junction of this 18-mile branch line connecting the original Santa Fe Railroad mainline to its namesake city. The 18-mile branch line was at that time a tourist shortline between Lamy and New Mexico's capital. The Santa Fe Southern did not operate in 2013 and the old Santa Fe mainline is now part of the Burlington Northern Santa Fe Railroad.

By the time Grigbsy had his movie train together, steamed, and ready for work, filming of *Appaloosa* had already begun at various locations around the area. For the three-day train shoot on the Santa Fe Southern on October 8, 9, and 10, in 2007, the center of operations for the movie company became the parking lots between the old Santa Fe depot in Lamy and a restaurant. A small city of trailers for actors, wardrobes, and equipment filled the parking lots between the hotel and depot. Vans carried actors and crew out to the movie set during the days of filming.

LEFT: Reader Railroad steam locomotive, No. 2, is between Santa Fe and Lamy, New Mexico on the Santa Fe Southern Railway during the third and final day of filming of train sequences for the western movie, *Appaloosa* on October 10, 2007.

RIGHT: Horse wranglers and production crew wait for the next scene during the making of the movie, *Appaloosa*, on the Santa Fe Southern Railway on October 8, 2007. This set near Lamy, New Mexico was used for three days of filming.

LEFT: Steven Greathouse oils Reader Railroad No. 2 between takes while filming of the western movie, *Appaloosa*, on October 10, 2007. The movie train is just a few miles from Santa Fe, New Mexico.

BELOW: Extras and railroad crew trade lighthearted talk on the last day of filming of *Appaloosa* on the Santa Fe Southern Railway on October 10, 2007.

Appaloosa starred Ed Harris, Renee Zellweger, and Viggo Mortenson. The film was directed by Harris and also featured Jeremy Irons.

Grigsby's train crew consisted of Gary Bensman, Steven Greathouse, and Perry Phillips. Bensman is a steam preservation expert, mechanic, and locomotive engineer from Martinsburg, West Virginia. Greathouse is from Florida. He is a diesel mechanic and couldn't resist the chance to come west and fire a steam engine for the movies. Greathouse had worked on another Reader steam locomotive, No. 4, when that engine was leased to a Florida tourist railroad near his home for a couple of years. Steven's dad, Charles Greathouse , also joined the crew and served as night watchman for the train after driving one of the tractor-trailer rigs to New Mexico.

Baldwin Locomotive Works built No. 2 in 1907 for the Lufkin Land and Lumber Company in Texas and the locomotive has been part of the Reader Railroad stable since the 1970s. Bensman assisted Grigsby in preparing No. 2 for another movie production, *There will be Blood*, in 2006

During the filming of *Appaloosa* train sequence, the Lamy restaurant served as a commissary, dressing rooms, and makeup areas for the film extras. Not only did the Reader crew provide and operate the train, they also suited out in western wardrobe for in case they were visible in the background. Grigsby dressed out as the conductor of the train. Bensman and Steven Greathouse donned vintage clothing as engineer and fireman and Perry Philips was decked out with a bowler hat and black vest for his part as the brakeman. A visit to the make-up department ensured that the men had the proper sooty, weathered look of 1880s railroaders. About a mile north up the line from Highway 285, the movie company built a water tank north of a small trestle.

"Hi, I'm Ed Harris," said the director and star of the film as he greeted the steam crew the first morning of filming. Dressed in black pants, a long black coat and black hat, Harris seemed poised as he began an intense three days of directing and starring in a western movie using a steam train from Arkansas. Movie making is a collaborative effort and Harris had lots of help from all of the other specialists needed to make a movie on location.

When Bensman and Greathouse warmed up the engine for the day's work by taking the train out on the line the first morning, a camera unit recorded interior detail shots of the locomotive cab. During this time Grigsby and the directors met to discuss safety issues and communication while working around an active, moving steam train.

ABOVE: Steven Greathouse walks on top of the tender of Reader Railroad No. 2 during filming of *Appaloosa* on October 9, 2007.

OPPOSITE PAGE, TOP RIGHT: Actor Viggo Mortenson sits in an open boxcar on the set of the movie, *Appaloosa*, on October 10, 2007.

OPPOSITE PAGE, TOP LEFT: Locomotive No. 2 is taken out on the Santa Fe Southern Railway for the first day of filming of *Appaloosa* in northern New Mexico on October 8.2007.

OPPOSITE PAGE, LOWER: The historic Santa Fe depot in Lamy, New Mexico is served by Amtrak's *Southwest Chief* twice daily. A streamline passenger coach serves as offices for the Santa Fe Southern Railway on October 9, 2007.

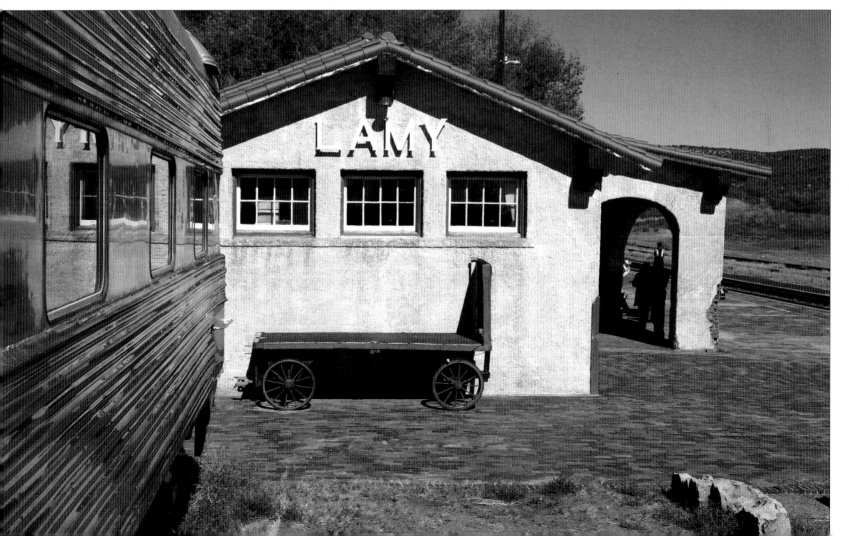

Left: Actor Viggo Mortenson, center, surveys the scene from the Reader Railroad boxcar during a break in filming of the western movie, *Appaloosa*.

Far Left: Steven Greathouse, fireman on the movie engine, Reader RR No. 2, pulls the water tank into place during filming of *Appaloosa*.

Below Left: A woman in costume acting as an extra in the movie, *Appaloosa*, sits in the coach of the Reader Railroad's movie train on October 10, 2007.

By the third day of shooting, only a secondary camera unit was left to finish a couple of scenes at the water tank. The rest of the movie crew had pushed on to other non-railroad locations. That afternoon the train ran at track speed for some long telephoto film shots as the sun sank low in the sky and illuminated the train and dark blue storm clouds that had just passed through the area. At one point a rainbow seemed to end over Santa Fe. Bensman later remembered that afternoon of as one of his most memorable moments of filming on the Santa Fe Southern. The high desert air, washed clean by rain, bathed the yellow sage and an Arkansas steam train with the magical New Mexico light.

After few days of rest, the Arkansas steam crew reloaded No. 2 and her tender onto trailers and prepared the coaches and boxcar for the road again. However their trip over the highways was short. They moved the train south of Santa Fe to the Ford Ranch, a location that is often used in western movies. Utilizing a mile of track and the western style buildings already there, the *Appaloosa* steam crew ran the train for several more days of filming the following week. Then Richard Grigsby's Arkansas steam train returned home to Reader, waiting for the next casting call to provide those unique images of the mode of transportation that made America great.

Above: Steam locomotive No. 2 from Arkansas' Reader Railroad is prepared by Steven Greathouse for the day's filming on the movie set of *Appaloosa* on October 9, 2007.

Left: Steven Greathouse, fireman on the Reader Railroad's steam locomotive No. 2, oils the engine in preparation for the first day of filming of *Appaloosa* in northern New Mexico on October 8, 2007

6 Harlowton, Montana and the Milwaukee Railroad: A Life on the High Plains

Barely 36 years have passed since the Chicago, Milwaukee, St. Paul and Pacific Railroad removed from service their durable electric motors that pulled freight and passengers over the Rocky Mountains from Harlowton, Montana to Avery, Idaho. Passenger trains like the Olympian and the Olympian Hiawatha brought passengers in first class comfort from the West Coast to Chicago through the rugged Montana wilderness. Catenary wires over tracks carried "juice" for the trains crossing the windswept prairies along the Musselshell River and through mountain passes.

Harlowton, Montana served as the division point on the electrified portion of mountain railway. Diesel locomotives from the east brought their trains into Harlowton and electric motors with their trolley-like hooks took over the trip west. The procedure was reversed on trains coming from the west.

RIGHT: The roundhouse of the Milwaukee Railroad remains in Harlowton, Montana and has been used as a hay barn after its abandonment in 1979.

BELOW: Milwaukee Road E57B is one of three surviving boxcab electric motors. This unit was built by General Electric in 1915 and retired in 1974.

Electrification of this line proved to be a good decision in 1914 when the harsh winters with subzero temperatures rendered the use of steam locomotives difficult in the rugged Rocky Mountains. Electric motors still seemed like a good idea even when they were removed from service in the mid-1970s. Fuel prices soared during this time of oil embargoes and lines at gasoline stations. Electrical power for the railroad came from the abundant hydroelectric power in the region. Abandonment of electric railroading progressed, and the catenary wires were pulled down and sold for scrap in the booming copper market of 1975.

Harlowton, Montana depended upon the Milwaukee Road for much of its livelihood. An active roundhouse, small yard and depot kept workers busy. The Graves Hotel just up the hill from the railroad provided lodging and food for travelers and railroaders. The Harlo Theater showed movies on Saturday nights. When electrification of the railroad ended in 1974, few people knew that the entire line would be gone by 1985.

In 1974, the last electric motor in service was General Electric E57B, a boxcab switcher built in 1915. The railroad donated the GE unit to the town of Harlowton and the engine sits today in the city park at the junction of US Highways 191/12 and Central Avenue North. A streamlined "Little Joe," a type of electric motor originally intended for shipment to Russia, is preserved at Deer Lodge, Montana, another Milwaukee Road town.

The Milwaukee Railroad still has architectural remnants in Montana that reflect the legacy of this once great railroad. Of course the road bed survives along the Musselshell River, but the track has been long taken up. The Sacajawea Hotel, built in 1910 in Three Forks, Montana, has recently been renovated and is operated as an upscale hotel. The Gallatin Gateway Inn in Salesville, Montana recently closed after a season as a classic hotel and restaurant. The Gallatin Gateway was an overnight stop for Yellowstone National Park visitors coming off trains from the mainline at Three Forks. One of the most impressive pieces of Milwaukee Road architecture remaining in use today in Great Falls is the Milwaukee Railroad station. This impressive two-story brick depot was last used by the railroad in the 1960s and has a 135 foot tower that looks over the Missouri River and the city. It is used today as an office complex.

LEFT: The Graves Hotel in Harlowton, Montana was built in 1909. The venerable hotel is closed at the time of this writing. Its wide veranda still commands a sweeping view of the Musselshell River.

Above: The builders' plate of General Electric No. E57B remains in place of the side of this Milwaukee Road boxcab motor E57B in Harlowton, Montana. This motor was one of the last in use on this railroad. The unit was retired in 1974.

Left: The Graves Hotel marquee with its peeling paint and rusting steel supports advertises a cafe and lounge.

LEFT: At the lower end of Central Avenue in Harlowton, Montana, the historic Graves Hotel sits on a hill overlooking the Musselshell River. The hotel is closed at the time of this writing, but the hotel and cafe accommodated Milwaukee Railroad workers in the 1970s.

BELOW: Metal lawn chairs line the veranda of the historic Graves Hotel in Harlowton, Montana and recall the glory days the Milwaukee Railroad.

A parade of railroad photographers made their way to Montana in the 1970s to photograph the last days of Milwaukee Road electrics. Two of the best were Richard Steinheimer and Ted Benson who both traveled to the state during the railroad's declining years. Benson remembers "blowing through town chasing trains," and spending the night in Harlowton in the late '70s.

I missed the remnants of active Milwaukee mainline railroading in Harlowton in 1975 when I moved to the Blackfeet Indian reservation to work as a physician. I wasn't interested yet in railroads and their history. All I wanted then was to ski mountains and paddle rivers. One route I drove from Billings, Montana to Great Falls took me through Harlowton. I regret not going down to the lower end of Central Avenue to explore the railroad.

In 2013 the old Milwaukee Road depot remains in Harlowton and is a Milwaukee Railroad museum. The roundhouse survives and has been used most recently as a hay barn. The roundhouse is on private property and not easily accessible. The depot has been restored and has new sidewalks and a new roof. A small industrial switcher sits outside among some other equipment beside the depot.

Movies are still shown at the restored Harlo Theater on weekends. The theater is operated by high school students as part of a school project. The Graves Hotel maintains a commanding view of the Musselshell River and the old Milwaukee Road shop sites and depot museum. Unfortunately, the hotel is closed after several attempts as a restaurant and hotel. The sweeping veranda has rusting metal lawn chairs inviting visitors on a good day to sit and remember what it might have been like to come up the hill off the Milwaukee Olympian Hiawatha and spend a night in this Montana farming community.

With the passing of the Milwaukee Road into history, Harlowton, Montana like many prairie towns struggles on into the 21st Century. Harlowton will always be remembered as an important junction on the Chicago, Milwaukee, St. Paul and Pacific transcontinental railroad where electric motors performed mightily, moving people and freight over the Rocky Mountains.

RIGHT: The Harlo Theater in Harlowton, Montana has provided weekend movie entertainment for residents of of Wheatland County since 1948. The theater today is operated by local high school students.

BELOW: A handcart rests on a short section of track at the former Milwaukee Railroad depot in Harlowton, Montana. Built in 1915, the depot today houses the Milwaukee Depot Museum.

7 The Strasburg Railroad in Lancaster County Amish Country

For the railroad photographer hoping to create landscape images reminiscent of the early 20th century, a fortunate coincidence of life occurred in Lancaster County, Pennsylvania. Time stood still in a way. The Amish settled in this region of Pennsylvania in the 1720s, and the Strasburg Railroad was chartered in Strasburg, Pennsylvania in 1832. A steam powered railroad and the Amish come together in a place that allows photographers the chance to create photographs that might have been made in the 1800s.

The Amish began as a sect of the Anabaptist movement in Europe after the Protestant reformation in 1517. Anabaptists were persecuted by governments of both the church and state for their practice of baptism of adult believers. In Switzerland in 1693, the Anabaptists split into two groups, the Mennonites and the more conservative Amish. The Amish, lead by Jakob Ammann, espoused the ideas of plain dress, hard work, devotion to a literal interpretation of the Bible, and shunning of those in the church who left the faith.

William Penn invited the Amish to migrate to America in the early 1700s as part of his experiment in religious tolerance in the New World. The Amish settled in Lancaster County, Pennsylvania in 1720 and became known as the Pennsylvania Dutch. Many are bilingual and speak a German dialect in addition to English.

Submission to God's will and humility are linchpins in Amish culture. They are known as the "Plain People," because of their unadorned clothing and simple living habits. Through their interpretations of the Bible and the Ordnung, their book of rules, Amish elders decide how the local churches and community respond to changing lifestyles and new technology. As a result, the Amish rejected automobiles years ago. They travel by horse and buggy. They eschew telephones and electricity in their homes because the use of these technologies might diminish the cohesiveness and morals of their community. The Amish still accept rides from their secular neighbors in automobiles or trucks for essential travel.

LEFT: Amish school children have walked into the picture during the passing of Strasburg Railroad No. 475 in Lancaster County, Pennsylvania on October 23, 2006. The steam train is being used for a Carl Franz sponsored photo session.

RIGHT: A driving wheel at the Strasburg Railroad shops is undergoing service on October 23, 2006. The Strasburg Railroad in Lancaster County, Pennsylvania repairs steam locomotives from around the United States.

LEFT, TOP: Strasburg Railroad steam locomotive No. 475 passes No. 90 during a Carl Franz photo session on the shortline in Lancaster County, Pennsylvania on October 23, 2006.

LEFT, BOTTOM: Late afternoon sun backlights steam and smoke from a Strasburg Railroad freight train on October 23, 2006.

BELOW: Early morning light illuminates the front of Straburg Railroad's No. 475 in Lancaster County, Pennsylvania on October 23, 2006.

The coming of the railroad to Lancaster County in the 1830s began the onslaught of industrialization that first threatened Amish life. Before the railroad, the Amish and their non-Amish neighbors, also called the English, lived similar agrarian lifestyles. They tilled the land on family farms true to Jeffersonian ideals. The railroad brought the first change to these isolated communities in Lancaster County and offered the new paradigms of American mobility and consumer culture. The rest of the U.S. and Canada moved into the 20th century; the Amish stayed focused on their beliefs and way of life from the 1600s.

In the 1830s the Strasburg Railroad was important in linking Lancaster County to the outside world. As passenger trains in the county declined with the advent of an interurban trolley service and automobiles, the Strasburg Railroad still provided important freight connections to other railroads through the 1950s. Due to declining freight revenues the owners sought permission in 1957 to abandon the shortline. Led by Henry K. Long and Donald E. L. Hallock, a group of investors purchased the Strasburg Railroad on November 1, 1958.

ABOVE: An Amish wagon passes a farmhouse in Lancaster County, Pennsylvania.

RIGHT: Storm clouds gather on the horizon as afternoon sun bathes Strasburg Railroad's No. 90 in light during a photo session runby on October 23, 2006.

The new owners found the line in deplorable conditions with some tracks completely buried under fields encroaching upon the right of way from adjacent farms. According to the railroad's website history, one of the new owners jokingly suggested they seek 4-H membership. After repairs and renovation, the first passenger train in forty years, pulled by a gasoline-powered Plymouth locomotive, left the Strasburg station on January 4, 1959.

The railroad soon bought a Canadian National steam engine No. 7312. It was renamed No. 31 and made its first run on September 6, 1960. Over the next twenty years, the railroad purchased five more steam locomotives. The Strasburg Railroad became a model for other shortline tourist operations around the country. The town became so well known for its tourist railroad that the Railroad Museum of Pennsylvania settled in Strasburg in 1975. This museum is situated across the highway from the Strasburg Railroad and is administered by the Commonwealth of Pennsylvania's Historical and Museum Commission. The railroad museum contains an extensive collection of railroad equipment, artifacts, and documents associated with the Keystone State.

Visitors to Lancaster County, Pennsylvania come from all over the world. They come to visit the Amish country that is known for a people who choose another way of life. There are somewhere between 16,000 and 30,000 Amish in Lancaster County with a total population of 250,000 in the United States and Canada. There are sizable Amish communities in Ohio, Indiana, Missouri, and New York. Each year, 20 million tourists visit Amish country.

Fifty years ago most Amish earned their living through agriculture. Today, only half of Amish men work on a farm. The other 50% are carpenters, furniture makers, and skilled craftsmen. Wives and children stay in the homes and when their husbands return from work, they all participate in the life of the church and the Amish community.

One reason for the decline in farming is there may not be enough land in Lancaster county for each Amish son to have his own farm today. There is intense pressure from the surrounding secular communities for this land and real estate prices have soared, pricing many Amish out of the market.

This conflict between the Amish who practice the old ways of living, resisting technology and change, reminds me of the conflict that railroad photographers of a certain age may feel today about the coming of the digital photography revolution. There are some who continue to shoot film and print in the darkroom, just as people have done for 150 years. There are other photographers who fully embrace the technology of digital SLRs, computer imaging, and digital printing. They have learned the latest Photoshop version and in many instances can make better prints from their desktops than they ever could in the darkroom.

The dilemma is this. What happens when the electricity fails or hard drives are corrupted and those images from 10 or 15 years ago cannot be accessed. The film photographer can pull out a sheet of negatives or transparencies, hold them up to the light, and say, "There's the photograph I made of Strasburg Railroad No. 90 in 2008." When our digital domain fails us, we may lose a large portion of our recent visual history.

If the oil stops and the world becomes chaotic, I know where I would like for my family to live: with the Amish, if they will have us. The Amish are survivors.

LEFT: A Strasburg Railroad mixed train performs a runby for gathered photographers during a Calr Franz sponsored photo session in Lancaster County, Pennsylvania on October 23, 2006.

ABOVE: The self-propelled railcar of the Strasburg Railroad has delivered a group of photographers into the countryside of Lancaster County, Pennsylvania where they await a photo run by of a special steam powered freight train.

RIGHT: A Pennsylvania Railroad GG1, No. 4800, is preserved at the Railroad Museum of Pennsylvania in Strasburg, PA.

8 Izaak Walton Inn: Historic Great Northern Railroad Hotel in Northern Rockies

Nestled in the northern Rocky Mountains, the Izaak Walton Inn is one of the few places offering a comfortable night's lodging between Cut Bank and Columbia Falls, Montana in the winter. That is a distance of only 118 miles, but when the snow flies and you are driving, it becomes a true wilderness experience. From October until May the great hotels in Glacier National Park are closed. Many of the motels in East Glacier, MT are open only in the summer. The Izaak Walton Inn provides an oasis of warmth with a soft bed and good food in the white expanse of prairie and mountains just south of the Canadian border.

In addition to serving those coming by automobile, the Izaak Walton Inn also plays host to passengers arriving twice daily by train. For over 100 years passenger trains with names like the Oriental Limited, Western Star, and Empire Builder have passed through these mountains on the old Great Northern transcontinental railroad between Seattle, WA and Minneapolis-St. Paul, MN. Today's version of the Empire Builder retains the name of its Great Northern predecessor, but is operated by Amtrak. Today's Empire Builder continues east to Chicago after leaving the Twin Cities.

BELOW LEFT: A Red Coach open-air tour bus is parked in front of the Izaak Walton Inn in northern Montana during a regular stop in the summer of 2011.

BELOW: Southern Pacific No. 4449 powers a train in a historic run over the Burlington Northern Santa Fe Railroad line on October 17, 2009. The train has stopped in front of the Izaak Walton Inn adjacent to Glacier National Park in northern Montana.

LEFT: Amtrak's Empire Builder arrives in Whitefish, Montana at the western border of Glacier National Park. The train made a brief stop at the Izaak Walton Inn before its arrival. The passenger train is westbound to Seattle, WA.

The Izaak Walton Inn is located in the tiny whistle-stop community of Essex, Montana about half way between East Glacier and Belton, MT. Essex sits on a hill above the Middle Fork of the Flathead River and U.S. Highway 2. This major east-west highway winds through the mountains after crossing the Continental Divide at Marias Pass.

It is only natural that the Burlington Northern Santa Fe Railroad's route across northwestern Montana attracts railroad enthusiasts to this hotel. Outdoor lovers of all kinds come to Essex because the small community is surrounded by the mountains of Glacier National Park and Flathead National Forest. There are few places better suited to spend the night, especially in the depths of winter, than the Izaak Walton Inn. There seems to be something for everyone with cross-country skiing in the winter, hiking and rafting in the summer, and photography at any time of the year. The hotel is situated against a spectacular mountain backdrop of big-time railroading for those who love to watch and photograph trains.

Larry and Lynda Vielleux have lived in Essex since 1982 when they purchased the Izaak Walton Inn. Originally from Big Sandy, Montana, the couple didn't ski that much or have any interest in railroading or historic preservation before buying the hotel. Larry Vielleux attended college at the University of Montana in Missoula, and had a fraternity brother, Larry Goodrich. Goodrich's father and mother, Sid and Millie Goodrich, bought the Izaak Walton Inn in 1972 and built their business catering to the needs of cross-country skiers. The Goodrichs reversed the slow decline of the hotel during their ownership by making the old railroad hotel into a cross-country ski lodge. Due to Sid's poor health in late 1982, the Inn had to be sold.

As owners of such a historic hotel, the Vielleux learned a lot from those early days in the cross-country ski lodge business. Much of that education has been about railroading and the relationship of their historic hotel to the Great Northern, now BNSF, mainline. The BNSF was the result of a merger of the Great Northern, Burlington, Northern Pacific, and Santa Fe lines along with several other railroad from 1971 through 1996. Framed calendars and photographs from the GN's publicity department of the 1940's and '50's decorate the walls of the inn.

James J. Hill founded the Great Northern Railroad in the late 1880's. Louis Hill, his son and successor, supported an alliance between conservationists and the U.S. government that resulted in the formation of Glacier National Park in

RIGHT: Amtrak's eastbound Empire Builder is approaching Browning, Montana on the Burlington Northern Santa Fe Railroad. The Rocky Mountains are left behind as the train has crested Marias Pass and emerged onto the prairie.

1910. To accommodate the flood of expected visitors, a GN subsidiary, the Glacier Park Hotel Company, built four magnificent lodges and a number of smaller chalets and cabins in the new park. The railroad provided transportation for Americans to see the glories of the Rocky Mountain west.

Essex, Montana originated because of the need for helper engines to shove freight trains over the continental divide. The new railroad penetrated the area of Essex Creek in 1890. A post office gave the community its identity in 1891. The first lunchroom and hotel were built in 1909. Both this hotel and its successor, the Red Beanery, burned.

In 1935 the National Park Service planned a new road that would leave U.S. Highway 2 and bisect the southern half of Glacier Park. Joining the recently built, spectacular east-west road, "Going to the Sun Highway," in the middle of the park, this proposed north-south road would need new accommodations

BELOW: A cosmetically restored EMD F45 passenger locomotive has been painted "Big Sky Blue" in the Great Northern paint scheme and lettered as No. 441. The locomotive shell has been outfitted inside for a guest suite at the historic Izaak Walton Inn in northern Montana. The diesel locomotive orignially started life as a Santa Fe Railroad unit.

for tourists at its southern terminus near Essex. A small hotel would also provide housing for train crews. The idea for the Izaak Walton Inn was born.

Looking north to the wilderness of Glacier National Park it is easy to imagine the road that never materialized yet was responsible for the construction of the inn. The Great Northern Railway competed the Tudor-style Izaak Walton in 1939. The highway north through the park was never built as World War II consumed the interest of the nation.

With only 33 rooms, the Izaak Walton was not designed on the grand scale of the Great Northern's other lodges in Glacier National Park. The Izaak Walton Inn became comfortable in its own way. From the beginning, the hotel was intimately connected to the railroad. That point of interest continues to this day.

Train crews still find their way to the hotel dining room that looks out over the upper end of the Essex yard. Railroaders take their meals and breaks at tables next to cross-country skiers and tourists. The railroaders' portable radios crackle with static and tell of approaching BNSF freights needing helper service up Marias Pass.

ABOVE: Southern Pacific steam locomotive No. 4449 is eastbound during a brief stop at the Izaak Walton Inn in northern Montana on October 17, 2007.

The last Burlington Northern Empire Builder stopped at the Essex depot in 1971. After several years of petitions, the Izaak Walton Inn owners finally persuaded Amtrak in 1986 to include Essex as a flag stop. Passengers now detrain on the east end of the yard to prevent their crossing several sets of tracks. Unfortunately the railroad razed the white depot building across the busy mainline. An Izaak Walton van meets the new Amtrak Empire Builder 300 yards east of the former depot. The Essex stop has become popular for passengers from both Seattle and Chicago and towns in between. Where else can you step off your Amtrak sleeping car and cross-country ski miles of groomed trails.

The Empire Builder is a big event each day at Essex. Activity quickens in the lodge as train time draws near. A standing rule for hotel employees is to wave at Amtrak when it passes. Rarely does a passenger train go by that someone from the hotel does not run out front for a greeting.

There was one time when an Amtrak dining car lost power and could not serve meals to passengers. The train crew called ahead and asked the hotel to have 400 sandwiches ready within two hours. All of the hotel guests went to work. Everyone rolled up their sleeves and got busy making sandwiches.

Lynda and Larry Vielleux retired and sold the hotel in 2005. The new owners appreciate the unique place that the Izaak Walton Inn has in Montana and railroad history. The hotel began placing renovated cabooses across the track near the inn's cross-country ski trails. Guests at the hotel

ABOVE: Amtrak's Empire Builder makes a regular stop at the Izaak Walton Inn in northern Montana. The cross-country ski lodge adjacent to Glacier National Park is popular with outdoorsmen, railfans, and tourists.

RIGHT: Amtrak's Genesis locomotive No. 826 has been placed on a siding in front of the Izaak Walton Inn in northern Montana. The diesel engine is awaiting inspection by crews after a minor mishap on an eastbound run in early 2000.

can choose to stay in one of these unique rooms if they choose. A new addition is also a renovated FP passenger diesel locomotive painted in the old Great Northern Big Sky Blue paint scheme. The locomotive has been gutted and replaced with a guest room inside for those seeking a different kind of experience.

After a day of skiing and photography, under warm blankets back in the hotel, the drone of a long freight rumbling into Essex lulls you to sleep. Although the cover of snow muffles sounds of the passing trains, strobes and piercing headlights silhouette men coupling helper units onto yet another train for the assault on Marias Pass. It is easy to imagine that come morning you might board a classic orange and green Great Northern streamliner for Chicago and the calendar downstairs might read 1939. Of course those days are past, but the illusion persists. Passenger trains still wind by snow laden peaks named for mountain men and Blackfeet warriors. Long freights struggle up the divide and railroaders still come over to the Izaak Walton for coffee.

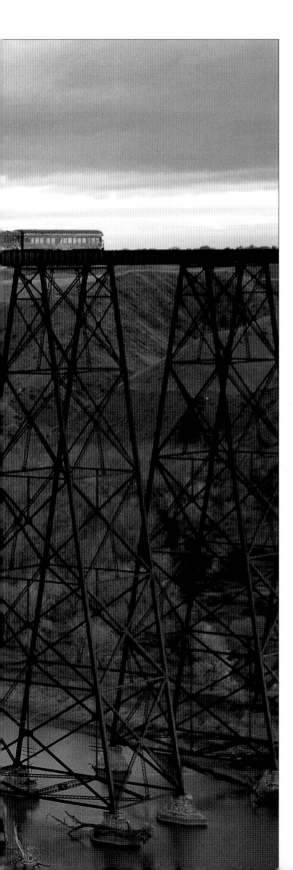

9 Canadian Pacific and the Lethbridge Viaduct

Sometimes things are more difficult than they appear. Canadian Pacific No. 2816 had just whistled for its departure from downtown Lethbridge, Alberta at 8:15 in the morning. I had driven north out of town on HW 3 and crossed the highway bridge over Old Man River. A glance to the left at the Lethbridge Viaduct, the highest and longest railroad bridge in the world, assured me there was no steam train yet. This soaring steel trestle is 314 feet high and spans the clear stream bearing a Blackfeet Indian name. The riverbank was lined with cottonwoods bearing the full glow of autumn's yellow colors.

Morning sun peeked out from below a large layer of overcast. Rain held off for the moment. Several times I had passed this high trestle in southern Alberta and hoped for a chance to see and photograph a steam train on the railroad bridge also called the High Level Crossing on the CP line to Calgary. I was about to miss it, though, because I didn't count on having to thread my way through a housing subdivision to find the edge of the coulee for a photograph of this rare occurrence.

LEFT: Canadian Pacific No. 2816 is headed north to Calgary after having just departed Lethbridge, AB on October 20, 2006. The steam train is crossing the Lethbridge Viaduct over Oldman River.

BELOW: Canadian Pacific No. 2816 steams north toward Calgary in a light rain on October 20, 2006.

ABOVE: A wooden tower stands at the corner of the Fort Museum in Fort Macleod, AB, Canada.

LEFT: Canadian Pacific steam locomotive No. 2816 in service outside of Lethbridge, October 19, 2006.

Scouting the location would have helped a lot, but my arrival into Lethbridge from Montana at midnight didn't leave much time for sleep or reconnaissance. I pondered for a time the view from the golf course on the valley floor but decided on the higher vantage point from the rim of the canyon. I finally found a parking spot and what appeared to be public space between the homes to lip of the canyon where I could gain a view of the trestle. RUN!

Cameras, tripod, and telephoto lens jostled in my vest pockets and on my shoulder as I ran. I made it to the coulee's edge and meet one other person, a railfan from England who had his point and shoot ready for action. We were not disappointed, and I made it just in time. The trestle is 5,331 feet, just over a mile in length. The steam train seemed to float in midair as it glided across this deep valley. A helicopter appeared over the trestle to shoot video of the event. Perhaps he was from a local Alberta television station. The chopper soon moved on and my English friend and I had the show all to ourselves. Where was everyone else, I wondered. Were they down on the golf course in the valley or perhaps on the other end of the trestle in Lethbridge?

ABOVE: The Grange Hotel still stands in 2006 in Carmangay, AB. Steam locomotive No. 2816 has just passed nearby on the way to Calgary.

OVERLEAF: Canadian Pacific No. 2816 rounds a curve near Carmangay, AB enroute to its home shops in Calgary. A light rain is falling as winter weather approaches on October 20, 2006.

LEFT: A Fairbanks Morse diesel, No. 4101, is stored in Ogden yards of the Canadian Pacific Railroad in Calgary, AB when this photograph was made in January 2006.

BELOW LEFT: A vintage pick-up truck is left to the elements on the prairie south of Calgary, AB in 2006.

Paul Bowles reminds us in the movie of his book, *The Sheltering Sky,* that because we don't know when we will die, we tend to think of life as an inexhaustible well from which we dip our experiences. Bowles tells us in a monologue at the end of the movie that there is a finite number of times we will see a moon rise or think back to a childhood memory. How easily we forget that this limit applies to our own lives. As I pack my gear and head for the car, I am thankful that just once I saw and photographed a steam train crossing the highest and longest railroad trestle in the world.

The High Level Crossing or Lethbridge Viaduct was 100 years old in September 2009. It still stands as the highest and longest railroad trestle in the world. There are no weight or train length restrictions on the bridge. John E. Schwitzer, who also constructed the Spiral Tunnels near Yoho National Park, was in charge of building this trestle. At the time of its completion, the bridge was considered one of the engineering wonders of the world.

10 Arkansas and Missouri Railroad: A Jewel of An Ozark Short Line

In 1986 the Burlington Northern Railroad, formerly the Frisco, sold their 139-mile route of between Fort Smith, Arkansas and Monett, Missouri to the newly created Arkansas and Missouri Railroad. In the years ahead the shortline railroad would play host to movie makers, politicians, and legions of train enthusiasts from around the globe. In just a few short years the A&M would become a jewel of a railroad in the heart of the Arkansas Ozarks.

Tony Hannold moved from Maryland to serve as president of the new operation. Hannold brought with him an all-Alco fleet of locomotives: Alco C-420s, C-424s, T-6s, one RS-32 and one RS-1. Headquartered in Springdale, Arkansas, the mountain railroad immediately attracted attention from railfans nationally because of these vintage diesel engines.

Alco locomotives on the A&M, with their distinctive appearance and 4-axle trucks, performed well for the short line. When tackling the 2.5 % grades of the old Frisco line through the Boston Mountains, the A&M used multiple units, sometimes as many as five or six, to hoist freight tonnage over the pass and through the tunnel at Winslow, Arkansas.

Most of the A&M Alcos were built in the 1960s by the American Locomotive Company in Schenectady, New York. By the time they came to the A&M, the units might have qualified for antique license plates had they been automobiles. Because of their unique design and vintage heritage, railfans viewed the A&M and Springdale as the Alamo for Alcos.

The Arkansas and Missouri Railroad appeared on the national map in 1987 when Universal Studios picked Fort Smith, Arkansas and the railroad for filming of the Neil Simon play and screenplay, *Biloxi Blues*. Don Primi, a New York train coordinator, brought Savannah and Atlanta No. 750 from Georgia and a string of former Erie-Lackawanna commuter coaches to the fledging short line to film this major motion picture.

LEFT: The excursion passenger train of the Arkansas and Missouri Railroad passes a country grade crossing in Crawford County, Arkansas on November 3, 2006. The train is southbound returning to Van Buren, AR from a trip to Winslow, AR.

RIGHT: Canoeists hold in eddys on Frog Bayou as the Arkansas and Missouri Railroad passenger train crosses a trestle in the Ozark Mountains. The train is northbound from Van Buren to Winslow, AR.

For eight days, residents and railfans got a look at what life might have been like in the 1940s as the train steamed through the Ozark mountains over the most scenic section of the old Frisco line. The opening and closing of the movie featured No. 750 and the train crossing the Arkansas River bridge from Van Buren to Fort Smith. Footage in the movie included shots on the trestles over Frog Bayou and night shots at Chester, Arkansas. Antique cars of the 1940s and actors in period costumes completed the period look for the movie. Footage from this week of filming in Arkansas with S&A No. 750 has also appeared in movies like *Seabiscuit* and *Fried Green Tomatoes*.

With the enthusiasm generated by *Biloxi Blues*, residents of western Arkansas hoped a passenger train might someday return to this new railroad. Hannold appreciated railroad history and photography. He drove a Volvo painted the same burgundy color as the A&M's locomotives. Hanging on his office wall in Springdale was a vintage photograph of a steam train along a river on the Boston and Maine Railroad. Hannold understood the unique status of his all-Alco railroad.

I remember Hannold stating one day in the early 1990s, "I'm too busy running a freight railroad," when he was asked about the possibility of operating passenger trains on the A&M. Hannold ran his freight railroad well. Service to his customer base increased and the A&M became a part of the booming Northwest Arkansas economy that included retailing giant, Walmart, and poultry producers like Tysons and Georges.

RIGHT: Roger Bice drives his restored 1937 Chrysler over the grade crossing at Winslow, Arkansas as the Arkansas and Missouri Railroad passenger train prepares for return to Van Buren, AR.

LOWER RIGHT: A television crew is filming footage on the Arkansas and Missouri Railroad for a segment on *Tracks Ahead* on National PBS stations. A vintage restored Yellow Cab and the A&M passenger train are included in the footage on June 2, 2010.

BELOW: Students gather on the platform of the Arkansas and Missouri Railroad after a benefit dinner train for the Fort Smith Trolley Museum on the evening of May 2, 2009. The students served meals to patrons on the train.

The public interest in passenger service persisted. In 1989, Sean Reed and Robert McClanahan brought a light weight streamliner train to the railroad from central Arkansas for a couple of years. The A&M provided locomotives and crew to power the weekend excursions over the A&M. The streamlined train even boasted a rounded-end dome observation car, the Susacapejo. Eventually the streamlined train of Reed and McClanahan was moved back to central Arkansas and Hannold began the railroad's own excursion service using a mix of renovated heavyweight passenger cars. Today passenger trains on the A&M may have a former California Zephyr streamlined dome coach, a caboose, and an open air car. The passenger trains of the A&M are popular. From April through November the passenger trains

run from Springdale to Van Buren two to three days per week. During the Christmas season in December, the A&M operates local children's trains inspired by the movie, *Polar Express*.

Politicians on the campaign trail love speaking from the back of an open platform observation rail car. They can come out of their private quarters on the coach, address a crowd of people and then move on down the line to their next campaign stop. In 1990 Governor Bill Clinton ran for re-election in Arkansas. On October 4 that year, just before the November vote, Clinton and his wife, Hillary campaigned by train from Fort Smith to Rogers, Arkansas deep into the heart of Republican territory.

"I tried to find a book of Harry Truman's train speeches, but couldn't, so I'll have to use my imagination," said Clinton as his train left Fort Smith. The campaign special used Reed and McClanahan's streamline coaches and Tony Hannold's private heavyweight business car, Traveler, on the rear of the train. Crossing the Arkansas River at Fort Smith the train stopped at the historic Frisco depot on Main Street of the river town of Van Buren, Arkansas. After a whistle stop in Chester, Arkansas, the Clinton campaign special stopped in Fayetteville, Arkansas at the former Frisco depot on Dickson Street near the University of Arkansas campus. Clinton greeted many of his old friends and colleagues in Fayetteville and the train pushed on to Springdale and Rogers.

Bill Clinton later sent Tony Hannold a letter thanking him for one of the finest days of campaigning he had ever experienced. After Clinton became President of the United States, I wondered if he remembered that good day of campaigning by rail in the Ozarks.

ABOVE: The excursion train operated by Robert McClanan and Sean Reed in 1989 crosses the trestle at Lancaster Bridge over Frog Bayou in Crawford County, AR. The track and locomotives for the train are leased from the Arkansas and Missouri Railroad in this precursor to regular passenger excursions by the A&M in the early 1990s.

LEFT: The Arkansas and Missouri Railroad passenger train crosses one of three high steel trestles deep in the Boston Mountain section of the Ozarks on August 15, 2012. A production crew is filming footage of the train for the Arkansas Department of Parks and Tourism for promotional television advertising.

In 1998 Arkansas Governor Mike Huckabee organized a campaign train that was well attended in the same communities as Clinton eight years earlier. By this time Hannold had retired and Larry Bouchet served as president of the railroad.

A big message of the Huckabee train in Van Buren was that the popular excursion trains on the A&M had been salvaged and would continue the next year. For a time it had appeared that passenger service on the A&M might be stopped. After meetings between Bouchet, Van Buren Mayor John Riggs, and Governor Huckabee, an agreement was reached to continue the passenger excursion service.

Other movie productions have used the railroad through the years including a remake of the Frank and Jesse James story and a World War II piece, *The Tuskegee Airmen*. Public television programs about trains in America have also featured the A&M.

Change continues on the Arkansas and Missouri Railroad. In 2013 the railroad announced the purchase of three EMD SD70ACE locomotives. These three SD70 ACEs will replace up to eight individual Alco C-420 locomotives on the daily freight runs to Monett and Fort Smith from Springdale. Does this spell the demise of Alcos on the A&M? That is unknown in 2013. But equipment does not last forever. The Arkansas and Missouri Railroad is a working railroad, not a museum. For now, the Alcos will survive. They will be used on local trains, switching moves, and on the passenger service. Even with the new EMD locomotives in place, the A&M remains a jewel of a mountain railroad and Springdale is still the last stand, an "Alamo," for Alcos.

11 The Story of Two Railroads in North Texas: The Grapevine and Museum of the American Railroad

Texas is a large state with few navigable rivers. Railroads proved vital to getting cattle, cotton, and oil to a market hungry for these commodities. Passenger trains with names like the Texas Special, Bluebonnet, Sunset Limited, and Texas Eagle brought travelers to the state and took sons and daughters off to college, war, and new jobs.

Texas boasts of a number of railroad museums and operating tourist trains to remind us of the rich heritage that exists in the Lone Star State. Two of the best railroad museums are in the Dallas-Fort Worth Metroplex. The Grapevine Vintage Railroad operates over the old Cotton Belt line, now the Fort Worth and Western Railroad, from Grapevine into the stockyards of Fort Worth, Texas. The Museum of the American Railroad started life as the Age of Steam Museum in Fair Park in Dallas, Texas and has just completed the move to its new home in Frisco, Texas.

The Grapevine Vintage Railroad runs passenger trains powered by both steam and diesel locomotives. This tourist railroad obtains trackage rights from the busy Fort Worth and Western. One unique feature of the Grapevine Vintage Railroad is that the excursion rail service is owned by the city of Grapevine, Texas. Originally started by the FWWR, the steam train was called the Tarantula Train in those early days because a map of the Fort Worth and Western Railroad looked like a spider's body and legs.

Grapevine is a small town with an historic main street that has been preserved and is lined with art galleries, restaurants, and antique stores. The city built an elegant Convention and Visitors Bureau across the street from the restored Cotton Belt depot and the facilities of the railroad. The two-story building with a five-story tower looks like a Victorian train station that might be 120 years old instead of a modern structure.

RIGHT: Grapevine Vintage Railroad steam locomotive No 2248 has recently been repaired and is under steam at the time of this photo from the shops in Grapevine, Texas on May 23, 2013.

RIGHT: Grapevine Vintage Railroad steam locomotive No. 2248 is undergoing repairs in the shops at Grapevine, Texas on April 25, 2012.

LEFT: The passenger train for the Grapevine Vintage Railroad is serviced in the exursion train's yard in Grapevine, Texas on the Fort Worth and Western Railroad.

ABOVE: The drumhead for the Grapevine Vintage Railroad is carried on the rear of an open platform coach in Grapevine, TX on May 23, 2013.

The Grapevine Vintage Railroad steam train is powered by a Southern Pacific No. 2248, a 4-6-0, ten-wheeler, that was built in 1896. The railroad also uses a 1953-era GP-7 diesel, for motive power. The diesel often runs the excursion trains and proved invaluable when the steam engine needs repairs. The railroad has four enclosed Pullman coaches with heating and air conditioning and two open-air coaches that can be winterized.

On static display at the western end of the railroad's property is Southern Pacific No. 771. During its working days this Mikado class locomotive ran on the Texas and New Orleans subsidiary of the SP. Built by Baldwin Locomotive works in 1913, No. 771 was retired in the 1950s. The Grapevine Vintage Railroad acquired No. 771 from the city of Victoria, Texas in 2006.

Twenty-five miles to the northwest in the city of Frisco, Texas, the Museum of the American Railroad is taking shape at its new home north of Dallas. The Museum started life in 1963 as an exhibit for the State Fair of Texas. Joseph Rucker, Jr., assistant general manager of the Texas State Fair and Dallas philanthropist, Everett DeGolyer, Jr., worked together to extend that exhibit's presence and the railroad museum at Fair Park became a reality. The display was called the Age of Steam Museum. The Southwest Railroad Historical Society cared for the growing collection of vintage railroad equipment. Important additions to the museum included a Union Pacific Big Boy and an Amtrak GG-1 that originally served on the Pennsylvania Railroad.

In 1987, the City of Dallas Parks and Recreation Department took over management of the museum. It was now possible for the Age of Steam Museum to be open to the public on a daily basis throughout the year. The museum hired several more staff and began cosmetic restoration of the assembled rolling stock. In 2006 the museum changed its name to the Museum of the American Railroad reflecting its expanding roll in education of the public.

RIGHT: Santa Fe F-unit No. 49 is a colorful part of the collection of the Museum of the American Railroad. This photograph was made in Dallas, TX at Fair Park just before the move to the museum's new location in Frisco, TX.

BELOW: A valve wheel is preserved on a historic piece of railroad equipment in the Museum of the American Railroad.

The Age of Steam Museum ran out of room at Fair Park. They also needed covered space to protect their valuable and growing collection of locomotives and rail cars. In 2007 the city of Frisco, Texas, a rapidly expanding community in the north Dallas area, approached the museum about moving to their town. The museum broke ground for its new home in Frisco in 2011. As of this writing, all of the equipment has been moved from the Fair Park location to Frisco. The new museum is still not open in late 2013. Work is said to be progressing well according to the organization's website. When open, the Museum of the American Railroad promises to be first class.

LEFT, ABOVE: Frisco steam locomotive No. 4501, a northern type, is on display at the old Fair Park location in Dallas, TX on August 18, 2011 before the move to the new Museum of the American Railroad location in Frisco, TX.

RIGHT, ABOVE: The interior of Santa Fe Railroad parlor club car No. 3231, is open for inspection by visitors at the Museum of the American Railroad at Fair Park in Dallas, TX.

RIGHT, BELOW: Santa Fe parlor club coach No. 3231 –preserved by the Museum of the American Railroad.

LEFT, BELOW: The chief logo used by the Santa Fe Railroad embellishes the side of Doodlebug No. M160,

12 Raton, New Mexico, High and Lonesome

There she sits, high and lonesome – Raton, New Mexico, on the old original northern route of the Atchison, Topeka, and Santa Fe Railroad through New Mexico. Population in 2010 was 6,885. Elevation remains 6,680 feet above sea level. Coming from the northeast on Amtrak today, Raton seems to say "Welcome" to the romantic notions of railroad architecture of the Southwest. Left behind in Kansas and eastern Colorado are those sturdy brick depots that seem at home on the American prairie. At Raton, the traveler finds a vintage stucco train station built in the Spanish Mission Revival style that is so prevalent across New Mexico and Arizona. Welcome to the real Southwest.

The railroad line over the pass was once the site of intense competition between the Atchison, Topeka, and Santa Fe Railroad building west from Kansas through southern Colorado and the Denver and Rio Grande Railroad coming south from Pueblo, Colorado. Both railroads wanted to build over Raton Pass on the border of New Mexico and Colorado along this mountainous section of the Santa Fe Trail. One problem stood in their way, Richens "Uncle Dick" Wootten.

Uncle Dick was a Virginian who came west seeking his fortune in 1836. After several episodes of trading and trapping in the mountains of southern Colorado and northern New Mexico, Wootton bought land on Raton Pass on the Colorado side, built a hotel, and placed a locked chain across the trail. He charged a toll, each stagecoach was $1.50 and a rider and horse cost twenty-five cents, for passage through his place. Whichever railroad could get Wootten to give them rights to build over Raton Pass would control what some considered the most important mountain pass in the west.

LEFT: The tower of the Raton, NM Santa Fe depot gleams in the late afternoon sunlight on December 23, 2012. The rail line is owned by the present day Burlington Northern Santa Fe Railroad, but sees only two trains a day over the route to Lamy, NM.

RIGHT: The Santa Fe depot in Raton, NM is bathed by moonlight in the summer of 1988.

On the evening of February 26, 1878, both railroads had teams of surveyors on the D&RG train from Pueblo to El Moro, Colorado, the closest railhead at the time to Raton Pass. Neither group supposedly knew that the other was onboard. According to Stephen Fried's book on the Fred Harvey hotel and dining empire, *Appetite for America*, the Santa Fe team waited until the D&RG people had checked into a hotel. The Santa Fe surveyors then quickly and quietly rented horses and rode in the dark twenty miles to Wootton's hotel on Raton Pass.

The Santa Fe group wrangled an agreement from the old mountain man to build their rail line over Raton. They hired some young able-bodied men to ride with them up the mountain and begin building roadbed in the dark. Come morning, the D&RG team arrived and discovered they had been tricked by the Santa Fe. Pistols were drawn and words exchanged, but there was no gunfire and Wootton told the Rio Grande surveyors that his deal was with the Santa Fe and that was final. Within a year, the Santa Fe had a rail line over Raton Pass, but its 3.5% grade made it one of the steepest of any mainline in the country.

A year later the Santa Fe built a tunnel through the pass which exists today. The tunnel removed some of the extreme curves and switchbacks over Raton Pass in those early days. The Santa Fe won the battle for the best crossing of the Continental Divide and opened the path onward for their railroad to California.

For the next almost 30 years, the original Santa Fe line over Raton Pass was busy. The steep grades over Raton compelled the line to complete their southern transcontinental route known as the Belen Cutoff, a line from eastern Kansas down across Oklahoma and the Texas panhandle. After its completion in 1908, more freight traffic was routed over this southern part of the railroad reducing operating costs per mile. Most of the passenger trains stayed on the Raton Pass northern route. There was some freight traffic on the Raton line until the merger of the Burlington Northern and the Santa Fe in 1996 brought about a rapid reduction in freight service.

In the second decade of the 21st century, there are few trains except for the twice- daily Amtrak Southwest Chief running over the original northern Santa Fe route. At Trinidad there is a line that goes north to Pueblo. Southwest of Trinidad on the northern Raton Pass line all the way to Belen south of Albuquerque, there are only passenger trains. This fact has led to the stretch of railroad over Raton becoming one of the most endangered rail lines in the United States today.

LEFT: A Santa Fe F-unit, No. 347C, is preserved at the California State Railroad Museum in Sacramento, California. Santa Fe locomotives such as this one in the classic red and yellow warbonnet paint scheme pulled passenger trains like the Super Chief and El Capitan through Raton, NM in the 1950s and '60s.

The BNSF wants Amtrak to assume part of the cost of track maintenance over the section of track from Trinidad to Raton and on to Lamy, New Mexico, north of Albuquerque. Amtrak does not have the money. The future for this historic stretch of railroad is clouded.

Some railroad bureaucrats have talked of rerouting the Amtrak service over the southern transcontinental route through Oklahoma and Texas. This part of the Santa Fe had trains called the Grand Canyon and the San Francisco Chief in the 1950s.

If the Raton Pass line lost Amtrak, it is possible the whole 200 miles of the old line might be abandoned. Towns with historic stations like Las Vegas, New Mexico and Lamy might lose rail service to their communities that has been in place for over 130 years.

ABOVE: Amtrak's Southwest Chief arrives in Raton, NM on December 23, 2012. Freight traffic on the current day Burlington Northern Santa Fe goes through Amarillo, TX on the southern transcontinental mainline.

LEFT: The northern mainline of the former Santa Fe Railroad through Raton, NM is devoid of any trains but Amtrak's Southwest Chief in 2013.

RIGHT: The logo of the Palace Hotel is painted on a window of this historic lodging in Raton, NM. The hotel is closed as of 2013.

Las Vegas and Lamy were once key departure points for the Santa Fe Railroad guided tours called "Indian Detours," that took travelers into the Navaho and Hopi Indian country. The Fred Harvey Castenada Hotel in Las Vegas is one of several landmark buildings that would would be affected by the cessation of trains service through this town.

One other important function of the Raton, New Mexico depot is that it still serves as the arrival and departure point for thousands of Boy Scouts headed to the Philmont Ranch Scout Center each summer.

Twenty years ago before the BNSF merger, the rail yard at Raton had some semblance of life. There were some freight cars on the sidings and a couple of Santa Fe diesels were available if needed. For now, the railroad at Raton, New Mexico remains high and lonely.

ABOVE: Right: Amtrak's Southwest Chief has arrived in the eveining of December 23, 2012 at Raton, NM at the former Santa Fe depot. A bus connects passengers to the train from Denver, Colorado.

ABOVE: The arches of the Santa Fe depot frame the eastbound Southwest Chief and the lone Amtrak passenger boarding in Raton, NM on December 23, 2012.

RIGHT: Long shadows fill the portico of the Santa Fe depot in Raton, NM on the evening of December 23, 2012.

FAR RIGHT: The doors at the entrance to the old Palace Hotel in Raton, NM reflect evening light on December 23, 2012.

13 Frisco "Fast Freight" and Steam Locomotive No. 4003: Fort Smith Arkansas

"Fast Freight" became the promise of the Frisco Railroad in the middle of the 20th Century. To help move heavy tonnage over the Boston Mountains section of the Ozarks, the St. Louis-Southwestern Railroad, or the Frisco as it was also known, purchased USRA Light Mikado type locomotive, No. 4003, a 2-8-2, in 1919. The locomotive originally was intended for the Pennsylvania Railroad, but was rejected for some unknown reason. Railroads operated under government wartime control and when the Frisco was offered the chance to buy No. 4003, the railroad accepted. The steam engine pulled freight trains between Paris, Texas and Monett, Missouri.

American Locomotive Works built No. 4003 in March 1919 at a cost of $53,619 in Schenectady, New York. The Frisco at one time had 125 2-8-2s in their fleet. No. 4003 is one of eight surviving USRA designed steam locomotives in the country.

With the move to diesel power after World War II, the Frisco retired No. 4003 in 1952. In 1954, the railroad gave the locomotive to the Arkansas-Oklahoma State Fair board and the engine was moved into a prominent place at the entrance to Kay Rodgers Park, the regional state fair grounds in Fort Smith. The locomotive served as a stately monument to rail transportation for fairgoers every fall and to motorists along Fort Smith's Midland Boulevard. Generation of youngsters grew up remembering the era of steam power by the sight of this Frisco locomotive.

In 1999, the Fort Smith Trolley Museum secured permission from the fairgrounds' board to place the steamer on museum property downtown along the Arkansas River. The locomotive was donated to the museum. The only stipulation was that the museum had to pay for the cost of the locomotive's move.

RIGHT: Frisco steam locomotive No. 4003 is displayed at the Fort Smith Trolley Museum in Fort Smith, AR. The mountain type locomotive was donated by the Frisco Railroad the Arkansas-Oklahoma Fair in 1954.

RIGHT: The firebox door is open on Frisco steam locomotive No. 4003 at the Fort Smith Trolley Museum in Fort Smith, AR.

LEFT: Frisco steam locomotive No. 4003 is a Mikado type, 2-8-2, that pulled freight trains through the Ozark Mountains of Arkanss and Missouri in the 1940s and '50s.

ABOVE: Steam pressure gauges are preserved in the Frisco steam locomotive No. 4003 at the Fort Smith, Trolley Museum in Fort Smith, AR.

General manager of the Fort Smith Trolley Museum, Bradley Martins, remembers how the Swink house moving company of Fort Smith hoisted the locomotive and its tender onto wooden beams on heavy-duty trailers for transport. "It may have taken about two days to actually complete the move," said Martins. "But the movers worked for several days before that getting things prepared."

The 80-plus-year-old locomotive sits close to the trolley barn at the museum where the doors of the former Frisco roundhouse in Fort Smith protect the entrance to the museum's trolley barn. The steam locomotive's driving rods are on site and protected from the elements.

Frisco No. 4003 earned preservation status on the National Register of Historic Places on July 12, 2004. The locomotive is rare, only one of six USRA Mikados in the nation and one of only eight USRA type locomotives in the U.S.

The steam engine at the Fort Smith Trolley Museum joins several other pieces of preserved railroad equipment. Sitting near the locomotive is a distinctive Missouri, Kansas, Texas, or Katy Railroad, maintenance-of-way car that started life in 1938 as a chair car. The coach was converted to service as a diner-bunk car for the wreck crew on the Katy out of Parsons, Kansas before donation to the museum.

The Trolley Museum also maintains a 35-ton switcher, Maumelle Ordnance Works Locomotive No. 1, a Vulcan gasoline powered engine. One other locomotive at the museum is a diesel 44-ton switcher built in 1953, U. S. Air Force Locomotive No. 1246.

Three retired railroad cabooses are preserved at the museum. There is a red Katy caboose just behind No. 4003, cabooses in the Union Pacific and Burlington Northern colors.

The other main attraction at the Fort Smith Trolley Museum is of course the streetcars. Operating over just under one mile of track is No. 224, a car built by the St. Louis Street Car Company in 1926. This trolley originally served the Fort Smith Light and Traction Company, the city's streetcar service that ceased operation in 1933. After a challenge from his wife, historian Amelia Martin, Dr. Art Martin assisted by their son, Bradley, organized the Fort Smith Streetcar Restoration Association in 1979 to bring vintage trolleys to the city. The Fort Smith Trolley Museum resulted and the car barn was built in 1985.

OPPOSITE PAGE, TOP: Steam pumps on Frisco locomotive No. 4003 are intact, but do not function on the cosmetically restored engine.

OPPOSITE PAGE, LOWER LEFT: The right sided engineer's controls are in place on Frisco steam locomotive No. 4003 at the Fort Smith Trolley Museum in Fort Smith, AR.

OPPOSITE PAGE, LOWER RIGHT: The dome of steam locomotive No. 4003 has been recently lettered.

BELOW: The driving wheels of Frisco No. 4003 are painted white on the sides. Several pieces from the side rod mechanisms are stored in the shops of the Fort Smith Trolley Museum in Fort Smith, AR.

ROGERS

LEFT: The late Art Martin, MD operates Fort Smith Trolley Museum No. 224 on the museum tracks in Fort Smith, Arkansas. Martin was the driving force behind creation of the Trolley Museum in 1979.

RIGHT: Birney car No. 224 belonging to the Fort Smith Trolley Museum sits on a tight curve for pictures in the snow in Fort Smith, Arkanss on February 11, 2011. Frisco No. 4003 is present in the distance.

With the acquisition and renovation of No. 224, track and overhead wire were then laid in a section of old Fort Smith. The Fort Smith street cars are a source of pride for the people of this city on the banks of the Arkansas River. School children take field trips to ride No. 224 and explore Frisco No. 4003. The museum and streetcar rides attract visitors from around the U.S. The museum and especially the steam engine serve as backdrops for local photographers in wedding and portrait photo shoots.

Will Frisco 4003 ever see service again? Martin muses that the locomotive might run again if an individual or group comes up with the one to two million dollars needed and the skilled personnel who could restore the steam locomotive to operating condition. Part of that money would go toward building an adequate locomotive shop for the restoration. The current trolley barn would not be large enough for such a renovation. For now we are left with "ghost trains," reminding us of the days when steam ruled the rails between east Texas and southern Missouri on the Frisco and when city residents got around town by trolleys of the Fort Smith Light and Traction Company.

14 The Reader Railroad: From the Piney Woods of Arkansas, A Movie Queen Emerges

In the piney woods of south Arkansas, Richard Grigsby's Reader Railroad is seeing new life on the Hollywood big screen. Operated for years as a tourist railroad complete with an operating steam-powered sawmill, this former logging short line entered a period of slumber when the last excursion train pulled into the Reader, Arkansas station in 1991. Eventually the track linking the Reader Railroad to the outside world on the Union Pacific connection at Gurdon, Arkansas was removed. The encroaching jungle of Arkansas' deep woods enveloped station platforms, tracks and equipment.

In early 2005, Grigsby answered the call for a steam train for the major motion picture production, *There Will Be Blood*. The movie was filmed on location in Presidio, Texas. Grigsby rescued 1907 Baldwin-built mogul, No. 2, from the vines and rust and restored this "Ghost Train" to operating condition for a second life in cinema. After the success of the movie which earned an Oscar for Daniel Day-Lewis,

RIGHT: Reader Railroad steam locomotive No. 2 is undergoing repairs in the railroad's shops in Reader, Arkansas on August 21, 2007. The engine is being prepped for filming of train sequences in the western movie, *Appaloosa* in October 2007.

BELOW: Reader Railroad steam locomotive No. 4 is pulled into the shops of the railroad in Reader Arkansas. The steam engine has worn the lettering for the Dardanelle and Russellville Railroad in the past.

ABOVE: Rail car wheelsets line the grounds of the Reader Railroad in Reader, Arkansas in August 2007.

Grigsby's movie train hit the road for New Mexico and appeared in the films *3:10 to Yuma* and *Appaloosa*. After those three films the Reader Railroad movie train went to Granger, Texas for a cameo role in Paramount Pictures and Ethan and Joel Coen's remake of the classic, *True Grit*.

To move his train to these far flung locations in Texas and New Mexico, Grigsby and his crew winch Reader locomotive No. 2 onto a specially designed low-boy trailer and pull the load by diesel tractor truck over the highways to each filming location. Rubber tires and mud flaps are placed beneath each wooden coach of the train and a separate tractor truck pulls the resulting load. The locomotive and train are then placed onto the tracks of the movie production's host railroad at the film site. When filming is finished the railroad locomotive and coaches are moved back to Reader where the steam train joined the other slumbering equipment awaiting the next casting call.

Grigsby and his family have long been in the lumber business, but railroading has been in his blood since the 1970s when he purchased the short line railroad from Shreveport attorney, Tom Long. Long purchased the railroad in 1950 and under his ownership the Reader began appearing in major motion pictures. In 1966 a cast of emerging stars came to Reader to make the film *This Property is Condemned*. The movie starred Natalie Wood and Robert Redford. The screen play was written in part by Francis Ford Coppola and directed by Sydney Pollack.

The next movie, filmed almost entirely on the Reader Railroad, was director Martin Scorsese's first feature film, *Boxcar Bertha*. The movie, set in the Great Depression, drew fair reviews at the time of its release in 1972 from movie critic Roger Ebert and the *New York Times*. The film starred David Carradine and Barbara Hershey in some of their early cinematic roles.

BELOW: On April 19, 2010, Steven Greathouse (right) and an unidentified worker on the Reader Railroad attach cables to the locomotive tender of No. 2 as they move the piece onto a lowboy trailer. The movie train is being transported to Granger, TX for an appearance in the movie, *True Grit*.

ABOVE: A wooden shop building provides protection from the elements while locomotives on the Reader Railroad undergo repairs at Reader, Arkansas on August 21, 2007.

ABOVE LEFT: The belts and wheels of a steam powered sawmill are ready for service at the Reader Railroad in Reader, Arkansas in August 2007.

LOWER LEFT: A Ford pick-up truck has been outfitted as a high-rail vehicle on the Reader Railroad in southwestern Arkansas.

It was not until Grigsby owned the railroad that the Reader's trains began appearing in films with wider distribution. Steam locomotive No. 4, a Grigsby engine on loan down in Mississippi, played an important role in the movie, *O Brother Where Art Thou?* in 2000. Once Grigsby's trains became known to film producers and directors, he found a new life for his vintage equipment. *True Grit* was Grigsby's most recent film.

Grigsby is especially proud of his operating steam powered sawmill at Reader. The day in 2007 that I visited the short line, the state boiler examiner was there to perform one of the regularly scheduled inspections. Grigsby showed us around the sawmill and the inspector seemed impressed with the facility. One amusing note was the painted sign remaining in place at the sawmill from steam train days in the late 1980s. The sign reminded sawmill operators to cut wood to boiler length. "Thanks, The Fireman," said the sign.

The Reader Railroad movie train found new life as an excursion train when Grigsby moved No. 2 and its coaches to Tavares, Florida. The train operates regularly on the Tavares, Eustis, and Gulf Railroad as the the Orange Blossom Cannonball. The steam train runs between the Tavares depot in Wooten Park on Lake Dora. The original Tavares depot, built in 1888, burned a number of years ago. The TE&G built a new replica of the old depot in May 2013 for their passenger excursions.

Grigsby is excited about the new Florida operation and makes frequent trips between his home in Arkansas and Tavares. Several of his long-time friends who have worked in the movies operate the steam train in its new home. In some ways the new home for the Reader movie train resembles the piney woods of Arkansas. One major difference between Read, Arkansas and Tavares, Florida is the larger number of tourists to visit the railroad. Tavares is close to Disney World and Orlando.

Grigsby is ready for the next casting call by the film business. While he waits, he is having a new adventure running a steam railroad in Florida. His aging movie queen, No. 2, keeps in shape in Florida for her next movie role.

RIGHT: A Reader Railroad baggage combine coach is ready for travel over the highways to a movie locaton in August 2007. The coach has wheels attached beneath and the load will be hauled by a tractor truck.

BELOW: Reader Railroad steam locomotive No. 2 and its tender are prepared for hoisting onto lowboy trailers for transporation to a movie set in Granger, TX on April 19, 2010.

ABOVE: The steam powered sawmill at the Reader Railroad in Reader, AR remains intact.

RIGHT: A sign remains at the steam powered sawmill from the days when the Reader Railroad operated as a tourist railroad in the 1980s.

PLEASE CUT
WOOD
TO LENGTH &
STACK NEATLY
Thanks
The Fireman

LEFT: Amtrak's Empire Builder is eastbound as it stops at the former Great Northern Railroad depot in East Glacier, Montana.

RIGHT: A logo bearing a mountain goat was used by the Great Northern Railway and the Glacier Park, Inc. Transportation Red Coaches.

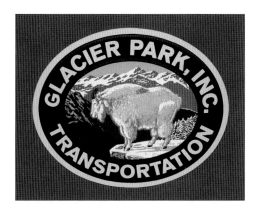

15 Trains to the National Parks: Glacier NP, Montana

Step off Amtrak's Empire Builder onto the station platform at East Glacier, Montana. Squint your eyes just right and imagine that the red, silver, and blue coaches of your train are Great Northern orange and green, and it might be easy to convince yourself the year is 1954 rather than 2014. The railroad hosting Amtrak's trains today is Burlington Northern Santa Fe. When you look west from the log depot at East Glacier, the scene looks much the same to the arriving train traveler as it did 60 years ago. A wide path lined by colorful flower gardens leads tourists up to the broad entrance of Glacier Park Lodge. A Blackfeet Indian teepee sits on the green lawn in front of the lodge. The Rocky Mountain Front with the peaks of Glacier National Park loom spectacularly behind the hotel.

Passengers disembarking from the Empire Builder may walk that hundred-yard path and leave their baggage at the station for transport to the hotel lobby. Or passengers and their luggage can ride one of the historic touring buses to the hotel. If there was ever a time machine to transport railfans back to the glory days of Great Northern Railway's Glacier National Park hospitality, arrival by train at East Glacier may be as close as it comes.

After Amtrak's Empire Builder whistles out of East Glacier, visitors to the park still enter a wilderness world knit together by a vintage system of lodging and transportation dating back to the Great Northern Railroad. In the early days of the 20th Century, railroads and boosters of America's fledgling National Park system promoted a campaign called "See America First." Glacier National Park celebrated its 100th birthday in 2010.

James J. Hill is called the "Empire Builder." because he pushed the Great Northern Railway across desolate high plains and through wilderness mountains from St. Paul, Minnesota to Puget Sound in the late 1800s. Hill's railroad opened the Great Plains to settlement and connected the resource rich Pacific Northwest to the Midwest and Eastern United States.

In 1912 when Hill retired from the presidency of the Great Northern he said, "Most men who have really lived have had, in some shape, their great adventure; this railway is mine."

If the railroad was James Hill's claim to greatness, his son Louis Hill took as his cause the creation of Glacier National Park when he ascended to the presidency of the railroad. When tourists arrived on Great Northern trains in the Montana wilderness in the early 1900s they needed lodging and food. Louis Hill gave them comfortable places to stay, a refuge in the northern Rockies that was only a generation away from the last of the frontier. Hill felt so strongly about seeing the new Glacier National Park become a reality with all of the amenities of home that he left his position as president of the GN to

LEFT: The streamlined train of the American Orient Express has stopped at the western entrance to Glacier National park at Belt, Montana on June 12, 2006.

OVERLEAF: Amtrak's westbound Empire Builder crosses the Two Medicine River at East Glacier, Montana. The mountains of Glacier Natiional Park on the Rocky Mountain Front rise in the background.

LEFT: The Morning Eagle is one of a fleet of vintage wooden boats on the high lakes of Glacier National Park, Montana. The Morning Eagle plys the waters of Josephine Lake in the Many Glaceir Valley. Mount Gould rises in the background.

BELOW: Amtrak station agents at East Glacier, MT meet the Empire Builder with a motorized baggage cart. East Glacier is the departure point for travelers coming by rail to enter Glacier National Park. East Glacier Lodge is a short distance to the west.

ABOVE: An eastbound Amtrak Empire Builder has just crossed the Continental Divide at Marias Pass and will soon stop at the depot in East Glacier, MT. The peaks of Glacier National Park rise in the distance along the eastern front of the park where the high plains meet the northern Rocky Mountains.

personally oversee the building of Glacier Park Lodge at the stop on the line called Midvale, Montana. This small community on the Blackfeet Indian Reservation, eventually renamed East Glacier, served as a portal to the new park and it still does today.

From Glacier Park Lodge the vacationer can tour the park without needing a car or other personal forms of transportation through the mountains. Red Jammers, also known as Red Coaches because of their color, are 17-passenger open-air White Motor Company truck type vehicles with comfortable leather seats that take visitors on scheduled tours throughout this mountain park. The Red Coaches can also deliver visitors from East Glacier to the other unique lodges in the park at Many Glacier Hotel, Lake McDonald Lodge, or Prince of Wales Hotel in the Waterton Lake section of the Glacier-Waterton International Park in Alberta, Canada. The 1930s-era Red Coaches have become an iconic part of Glacier National Park. When the touring buses were taken out of service for replacement of motor mounts from 2000-2002, they were replaced temporarily with Dodge vans. The Red Coaches' absence left a void. Many long-time park visitors felt something was missing on the roads in Glacier.

The drivers of the tour buses are called "jammers," because of their habit in years past of grinding through the gears of the unsynchronized standard transmissions as they climbed steep mountain passes. All of the Red Coaches have been retrofitted with automatic transmissions, but the "jammer" moniker remains for the drivers earning the right to captain a Red Coach for the summer. When the motor mounts were replaced in 2000, the whole fleet of 33 Glacier Park touring coaches were changed by the Ford Motor Company to run on cleaner burning propane gas.

Hikers hit the trails in Glacier can still find solitude. Canoeists and rafters float the North Fork and Middle Fork of the Flathead River and enjoy whitewater excitement and solitude. They may also see wildlife. A bluff outcropping of salt and other minerals occurs on the Middle Fork. Here paddlers may see Rocky Mountain goats. The "Goat Lick" is also visible by motorists from U.S. Highway 2 and from Amtrak trains on the nearby BNSF mainline.

Glacier National Park possesses several high mountain lakes. Hikers and sightseers often enjoy trips on a unique fleet of wooden boats operated by the same family for over 80 years. The Glacier Park Boat Company began with Arthur Burch, Sr. and Billy Swanson in 1938. Commissioned by the Great Northern Railroad, Burch and Swanson built a fleet of wooden boats that survives into this new century. These vintage boats with classic lines ply the waters of St. Mary's, Josephine, Swiftcurrent, and Two Medicine Lakes, and Lake McDonald under the care of Scott and Barbara Burch of Kalispell, Montana.

Settle into a comfortable bed at East Glacier Lodge after a week in the mountains. When you are ready to leave the next day, squint your eyes just right and that gleaming Amtrak train arriving from Seattle in the morning sun might just seem like the orange and green of the Empire Builder from the 1930s.

ABOVE: Swiftcurrent Lake provides the alpine setting for Many Glacier Hotel in Glacier National Park, MT. A Red Coach has just boarded a load of travelers for their trip through the park.

LEFT: A Red Coach trip through Glacier National Park in Montana provides a great introduction to the high alpine country in the northern Rocky Mountains.

ABOVE RIGHT: A Blackfeet dancer in traditional dress performs at the annual North American Indian Days in Browning, MT.

LOWER RIGHT: East Glacier Lodge is open only during the summer months and oftens serves as the first point of entry into Glacier National Park for travelers arriving by train.

LEFT: Amtrak's westbound Empire Builder passes a Burlington Northern Santa Fe Railroad freight train near Marias Pass on the southern border of Glacier National Park, MT.

16 Kansas City Southern Holiday Express

I owe Mike Haverty a debt of thanks for assisting in my ongoing quest to know why I have this life-long fascination with trains. Haverty, as president of first the Santa Fe Railroad and then CEO of the Kansas City Southern Railway, put form and substance to my distant childhood memories of Santa Fe Warbonnnets and Southern Belle streamliners. In the late 1980s while at the helm of the Santa Fe, Haverty brought back the most famous paint scheme ever applied to a diesel locomotive, the red, yellow, and silver Warbonnet attire made famous by the Super Chief and other Santa Fe passenger trains with evocative names from the American Southwest. Just as the New York Central Hudson became an icon of the steam era, the Santa Fe Warbonnet became synonymous with "streamliner" in the 1950s. Now as chief of the KCS, Haverty brings us a ghost of the Southern Belle, the classic streamliner that once rambled from Kansas City through the Ozarks and Ouachita Mountains down to New Orleans.

I once believed a Santa Fe Warbonnet to be most beautiful locomotive ever to lead a stainless steel passenger train. I may have changed my mind, thanks to Mr. Haverty. Several years ago I photographed the annual KCS "Holiday Express" as it visited much of the railroad's system during the month of December. It stopped at cities large and small, offering Santa Claus and a "Thomas the Tank Engine" look-alike for the kids. The real show for me was the newly painted F-units and the business train that pulled the Christmas service. The locomotives and coaches wore the newly applied authentic paint scheme of the Southern Belle streamliner.

BELOW: The Kansas City Southern Holiday Express is pulled into position as a young family watch. The special train is in Mena, Arkansas on December 6, 2012.

RIGHT: The Kansas City Railway recreates the Southern Belle of the 1950s as it brings the Holiday Express around the system each Christmas season.

As a young husband and father in the early 1980s, my family and I lived in Mena, Arkansas, a small town of 5,000 on the KCS mainline in the heart of the Ouachita Mountains. During those three years in Mena I often wondered what the venerable brick depot in Mena might have looked like with the Southern Belle pulling into town. I knew how the white SD-40 diesels with big red KCS lettering painted on their sides appeared as they passed through town by the scores on a daily basis. I could hear those freight trains five miles away on either end of town as they whistled for crossings. It was hard to make an SD-40 into a vision of the Southern Belle as it passed the old depot. Finally on December 5, 2009, as the Holiday Express eased past the station, I had the chance to know how 1957 might have appeared when a KCS train with the name of a beautiful woman pulled into the Mena depot.

ABOVE: The Kansas City Southern Railway's Southern Belle business train arrives at the depot in Mena, Arkansas on December 5, 2008.

OPPOSITE PAGE, ABOVE: The drumhead on the Southern Belle bears the classic logo of the Kansas City Southern Railway.

LEFT: The Southern Belle eases past the Mena, Arkansas depot on December 5, 2008. The Holiday Express Christmas train travels to communities each year.

OVERLEAF: The KCS Southern Belle business train pulls the Holdiay Express to towns and cities on the railroad each December. The train is south of Mena on December 5, 2008.

I had traveled earlier on that day in 2009 from my home in Fort Smith, Arkansas to Wickes, Arkansas, south of Mena. I waited for the Belle on the large sweeping curve coming into town. After only a few minutes the streamliner, with its unmistakable single chime horn, rolled around that curve. The business unit pulled the whimsical Christmas train in holiday dress. I was struck with the beauty of this business train's recreation of the Southern Belle. It seemed like a dream from my youth. The cartoonish Christmas train trailing behind delighted the kids at trackside, but my real interest was the F-unit diesels with their rounded nose cabs and black, yellow and red streamline train.

I photographed the northbound Southern Belle beside the twisting turns of two lane U.S. U.S Highway 71, which runs up the southwestern edge of Arkansas from Texarkana. I wanted photographs of the striking train at places like Vandervoort, Arkansas where the KCS tracks run by an old Masonic hall and a well in the middle of the road. But most of all I wanted a photograph of the Southern Belle as she pulled into Mena. After some quick shots about 8 miles south of town, I drove straight to Mena. A crowd of parents and children had already gathered to see Santa Claus and the "Holiday Express." They waited anxiously for the train's arrival. And so did I, but for other reasons.

LEFT: A member of the train crew on the Kansas City Southern Railway's Holiday Express coordinates train positioning at the depot in Mena, Arkansas on December 6, 2012. The business train will park the Christmas train in front of the depot for the next four hours.

RIGHT: The open platform observation coach of the KCS Southern Belle brings up the rear of the business train in Poteau, Oklahoma on December 8, 2011. The train has just dropped the Holiday Express into position on the mainline for the next four hours of visitation by children and adults of this eastern Oklahoma community.

The sun in the afternoon was bright and streaming straight down the track from the direction of the northbound train. I would be shooting into the setting sun if I placed my self across the track from the depot. I decided to go to the north end and photograph the train as the locomotives made their way past the open portico at the end of the depot. Fortunately for me, the city had removed the antique police car that usually sat under the covered north end of the depot. My camera had a straight shot through that now open area as the train slowly moved past the old station. I made a number of images of the locomotives and passenger coaches as they moved past. The train stopped and the Christmas unit was uncoupled. Then the business train moved down the track where it would remain until 8 p.m. But I had the photograph I had driven hundreds of miles to make. I had witnessed a genuine KCS Southern Belle at the Mena depot. Over the years since, I have photographed the annual Christmas train on the KCS pulled by their classic Southern Belle business train. But, I don't think I have ever made a better photograph of this train than the one on that day in December 2009.

I have visited Sacramento's California State Railroad Museum and seen the Santa Fe F-7 diesel locomotive preserved in the shiny paint of the classic red and yellow Warbonnet. I have seen Santa Fe locomotives bearing this revival paint scheme during the 1990s out in New Mexico and Arizona. And now I have seen the Southern Belle in all her glory. These are the trains of my youth. My personal pilgrimage has ended. Once these images existed only in my memory and in the books of photographers from another era. Now I have my own photographs of the trains that captured my imagination at a young age. I have a modern view of yesterday's icons. Thanks Mike Haverty!

The White River
Limited

17 American Streamliners

As America sank into the depths of the Great Depression in the early 1930s, unemployment hovered at 25%. Railroads felt the pain. The automobile had already taken away passengers by the droves in the preceding decade. The number of cars and trucks jumped from 8 million in 1920 to 24 million in 1930. Railroads found their freight and passenger business declining even more as people had little money for travel and fewer goods to ship.

In 1932 Ralph Budd, a civil engineer and railroad man, became president of the Chicago, Burlington, and Quincy Railroad. He joined the Burlington at the worst of the Depression, but he had a vision for helping lift the country out of the economic morass with new ideas in passenger trains. Ralph Budd knew railroading.

In Philadelphia, Pennsylvania, Edward Budd knew automobiles and had been experimenting with a new method of shot welding that attached stainless steel panels to car bodies. The two Budds had never met and there is a question about whether they were distantly related. They became friends and

ABOVE: Cedar Rapids, brings up the rear of a special steam powered special train on the former Burlington Northern Santa Fe line in Montana on October 17, 2009

LEFT: The dome-observation car of the Branson Scenic Railway is on the rear of the train as it crosses a high steel trestle on the Missouri and North Arkansas Railroad.

RIGHT: The skytop lounge observation coach, Cedar Rapids, brings up the rear of a special steam train powered by Southern Pacific No. 4449 on the BNSF in northern Montana on October 17, 2009.

began designing Burlington's first streamlined train, the Zephyr, using the emerging science of aerodynamics. Ralph Budd was convinced that a lightweight train could reduce operating costs and bring back passengers with this radical new modern design.

At the same time engineers under Averell Harriman on the Union Pacific Railroad built their own lightweight version of a streamliner. Drawing from their experience with the McKeen motorcars used in branch line service in the 1920s, U.P. engineers designed what became their first streamliner, the M10,000. Utilizing body construction by the Pullman Company and a gasoline motor from Electro-Motive Company, the M10,000 emerged with a locomotive that drew its styling from the automotive industry and pulled an articulated three car train. The entire train was painted Armour yellow and brown. The bulbous nose of the locomotive boasted a penetrating headlight that lit the track ahead and a vertical spotlight from the top of the locomotive to warn pedestrians and motorists at grade crossings of the fast approaching train.

Union Pacific won the race to complete the country's first streamliner. The M10,000 or "Little Zip," as the train became known, made its first test run on February 11, 1934. Thousands of onlookers turned out along the route and at stops along the way people lined up to tour the new train. The "Little Zip" embodied hope for the future through new engineering and scientific principles. The train toured the country and showed America the future of passenger travel.

On May 6, 1934, the Burlington's Zephyr made a record run from Denver Union Station to Chicago. Now two competitors in western railroading had streamline trains racing across the country. A revolution in both passenger travel and freight locomotives ensued. Diesel motive power was poised to replace the living, breathing steam locomotive loved by so many.

Soon the U. P. had multiple streamliners named for cities served by the new passenger trains. There were trains called City of San Francisco, City of St. Louis, City of Los Angeles, and City of Salina. The Burlington had their Zephyrs, named for the west wind. The Nebraska Zephyr, Twin Cities Zephyr, and Denver Zephyr moved passengers at unheard of speeds around their system.

Streamlining took hold of American's imaginations, especially after the two new streamliners, "Little Zip" and Burlington Zephyr, made their appearances at the Chicago World's Fair in the spring of 1934. Industrial designers began applying the streamliner look to all kinds of products like toasters, cars, buildings, and radios.

BELOW: The table is set in the streamliner dining car of the American Orient Express at East Glacier, Montana on July 12, 2006.

BOTTOM: A dining car attendant in the dome coach on the Arkansas and Missouri Railroad serves lunch to hungry rail travelers.

Some railroads were not certain that the diesel locomotive was reliable enough to trust with their name trains, so they put streamlining ideas to work shrouding steam locomotives in sleek stainless steel facades. Industrial designers like Otto Kuhler, Henry Dreyfuss, and Raymond Lowey developed rocket-like bullet nose locomotives for the New York Central, Pennsylvania, and Milwaukee Railroads. Soon most railroads had their streamlined trains, many still using stream power hidden behind streamliner make-up. The future became clear. Locomotives down the road would be diesel not steam.

President Franklin Roosevelt's New Deal brought relief to drought-ravaged America during the late 1930s and the railroads brought hope for a new world with their streamline trains. Then World War II got in the way. With the U.S. joining Allied Forces in the fight against Germany, Japan, and Italy, in 1939,

ABOVE: The dome dining car is set with crystal and china on the American Orient Express at East Glacier, Montana. Rail travelers on the train are arriving from a day spent in the mountains of Glacier National Park will will soon be eastbound toward eastern Montana.

manufacturers in America began producing material for the war effort. Edward Budd's Philadelphia factory began producing tanks and vehicles for the battlefield. Railroads carried thousands of soldiers across the country for deployment to the front. Loads doubled during the war years. Railroad equipment and personnel took a beating from the intensive movements of troop trains on the nation's carriers. Everyone felt stretched thin.

When WWII finally ended, railroad executives took stock of what remained, and the sight was not pretty. Everything was worn out. But they took courage from the optimism of returning GI's to civilian life. "We are all going to want to go places," said Edward Budd.

Ralph Budd at the Burlington planned a new streamlined train, the California Zephyr. This streamliner would be delivered from Chicago to California through the joint effort of three railroads. The Burlington took the train from Chicago to Denver where the Denver and Rio Grande Western moved passengers straight through the heart of the western mountains fulfilling their slogan, "Mainline Through the Rockies." In Salt Lake City, Utah, the train came under the care of the Western Pacific Railroad for the final leg to San Francisco.

ABOVE: A passenger boards the Union Pacific streamliner train in Cheyenne, Wyoming after a day spent at the Frontier's Day Rodeo. The train is the Frontier Days' Special that originated in Denver, Colorado in the morning. The UP Railroad brought Americans some of the first streamliner trains in the 1930s.

RIGHT: The classic streamline design of Southern Pacific's No. 4449 is evident as it steams past a sign announcing Walton Mountain on the BNSF line along the southern border of Glacier National Park, Montana on October 17, 2009.

The Burlington also pioneered the idea of the Vista Dome, a sleek passenger coach with an elevated glass-covered seating are running down the middle of the car. Cyrus Osborn at General Motors came up with the idea of the Vista Dome after he rode the cab of a diesel locomotive through Glenwood Canyon in Colorado. The dome cars were an instant hit.

Most American railroads in the 1950s boasted their own version of streamliners pulled by the powerful diesel locomotives produced by EMC. The Rock Island offered its Rockets. The Kansas City Southern Railway debuted its Southern Belle in 1940. The Missouri Pacific flew its Flock of Eagles. The Southern Pacific even shrouded a Lima-produced steam locomotive in 1941 and painted the engine orange, red, and silver to pull their fabled Daylights down the coastlines of California, Oregon, and Washington. Some called these SP Daylights, "The most beautiful train in the world."

The most recognized streamliner paint scheme in America became the red, yellow and silver of the Santa Fe Railroads' Warbonnet. The Santa Fe used a varied naming system for its special streamliners. The most famous was the Super Chief, an extra fare speedster between Los Angeles and Chicago. Other trains on the Santa Fe included the El Capitan, San Francisco Chief, and Texas Chief.

Even the bright new streamliners of the 1950s could not stem the tide of red ink suffered by American railroads during the 1960s. A fatal blow came for the revenue potential of the passenger train came when the U. S. Mail was taken off the railroads and moved to the highways or airliners. Railroads could not keep up with the public's romance with the automobile and air travel.

TOP RIGHT: An engraved glass in the door of the diner on the Rio Grande Zephyr advertises the Rio Grande Railroad as the Mainline Through the Rockies.

BOTTOM RIGHT: A streamliner observation coach brings up the rear of a steam special powered by Norfolk and Western No. 611 across Missouri in the 1980s.

In 1971, the nation's passenger service was nationalized with the advent of National Rail Pax or Amtrak as it became known. Coaches and locomotives from the participating railroads moved off their native lines into the far reaches of the country. A Union Pacific coach might show up on the east coast. A Pennsylvania locomotive might venture far afield from the Keystone state. Eventually this classic "heritage" equipment from the streamliner era began to wear out and was replaced with new Amtrak-designed coaches and locomotives. Vintage F-units and some worn-out E-units were returned to the participating railroads. Gradually these classic streamliner diesels, commonly called "cab" units were either scrapped, sent to short line railroads, and sold or donated to museums.

Admirers can still experience the glory days of the streamliner period by visiting museums or taking a ride on some of the stainless steel trains on tourist roads. Several freight hauling railroads maintain streamliner era business trains to ferry shippers and guests around their system. The Union Pacific maintains an exquisite fleet of E-Unit diesels along with their steam locomotives to pull classic lightweight trains across the west. The Kansas City Southern Railway renovated a diesel-powered streamliner in authentic Southern Belle colors and takes the trains around the system on its annual Holiday Express. Streamliners still offer hope for the future and remind us of our past.

BELOW: A streamliner dome car on the Arkansas and Missouri Railroad gives passengers great views of the Arkansas Ozarks between Van Buren and Springdale. Here the passenger train crosses Frog Bayou at Lancaster Trestle. The dome coach is originally part of the California Zephyr from the 1950s. The coach was first owned by the Western Pacific Railroad.

LEFT: Southern Pacific's No. 4449 displays classic streamlining as adopted by builders of steam locomotives in the 1930s and '40s. The train has come from Portland, Oregon to the 1984 New Orleans World's Fair. The train is readied for departure from Houston, Texas on June 10, 1984.

BELOW: On another excursion special, streamlined Southern Pacific steam locomotive No. 4449 travels the Burlington Northern Santa Fe mainline over Marias Pass along the southern border of Glacier National Park, Montana on October 17, 2009.

18 Kansas City Union Station

Kansas City Union Station opened my young eyes to the much larger world in which I lived in October 1958. This formative experience began when my grandfather drove my mother, brother, and me in his new 1957 Chevrolet Belair, from Fort Smith, Arkansas to Sallisaw, Oklahoma. We boarded Kansas City Southern Railway's Southern Belle and started the journey that took us far from our Ozark home in Arkansas to northern California .

According to the Official Guide of 1961, we probably boarded the northbound Southern Belle at Sallisaw, Oklahoma at 1:20 p.m.. I don't have a copy of the 1958 Official Guide, but I estimate these 1961 times are still close to what the schedule was in 1958. I don't remember much about about the Southern Belle part of the journey, but my world expanded and my eyes widened when we stepped off the train into the Great Hall of Kansas City Union Station. I remember the immense space that enclosed so many people. Most of all I remember the man from India in a vested suit, a Sikh I now understand, walking down the hall wearing a maroon turban headdress. Women in fur coats and high heels strode beside their husbands in gray business suits. That's the way people traveled in those days. There were soldiers in uniform hurrying for their next train. It seemed like all of the world had descended upon this one cavernous railway station.

Since we probably had about two hours to wait for our train west, the Santa Fe Railroad's San Francisco Chief, my mother probably took her two young sons to eat a meal soon after we got off the Southern Belle. There is a good chance we had supper in the Fred Harvey coffee shop in Union Station. I doubt that we ate at the more expensive Westport Restaurant also operated by the Fred Harvey company.

LEFT: Amtrak's Southwest Chief boards passengers at Kansas City Union Station on June 28, 2012. The bridge over the tracks gives pedestrians wide views of approaching trains. The bridge is accessed though Union Station.

Today I know much more about the history of Kansas City Union Station. As a ten year old boy, if I had looked up to the second floor offices of Union Station, I might have seen the doors to the corporate headquarters of the Fred Harvey Hotel and Restaurant empire in the American Southwest. Fred Harvey brought food and lodging to travelers along the Santa Fe from Chicago to California and his legendary company supplied all of the dining services on Santa Fe passenger trains. Union Station was home to this early 20th Century giant of the hospitality business.

We probably boarded the San Francisco Chief by 11:45 p.m. for that was departure time for the westbound Santa Fe streamliner. We awoke the next morning in the Texas Panhandle. I remember Amarillo, Texas and Clovis, New Mexico. Just as travelers on Amtrak's Southwest Chief do today, we passed through Newton, Kansas in the middle of the night. For a number of years I always thought we had traveled over the original Santa Fe route though Dodge City, La Junta, Colorado and over Raton Pass. Reviews of timetables showed that had we taken this northern route, we would have gone over Raton, then through Las Vegas and Lamy, New Mexico before arrival at Albuquerque, New Mexico. But my mother chose the San Francisco Chief which traveled the Santa Fe's southern transcontinental route through the Texas Panhandle and east central New Mexico. The northern and southern transcontinental lines separated just past the important junction of Newton, Kansas. The two routes of the Santa Fe joined at Belen, New Mexico just south of Albuquerque.

Traveling by rail through desert and mountains sparked my imagination. My fascination with the American West, railroads and history was a result of that trip. The genetic switch in my DNA that made me a rail fan had definitely been turned on.

What I remember most vividly is that passage through Kansas City Union Station for just a couple of hours. Returning to this iconic building in Kansas City today reminds me of when my life took a giant step forward into the future. Paris may have its Eiffel Tower, London has Big Ben, and New York City claims the Empire State Building but, Kansas City has Union Station.

FAR LEFT: Electric chandeliers provide illumination for Kansas Ctiy Union Station.

LEFT: A panoramic mural by Anthony Gude Benton shows the major railroads of KC Union Station.

RIGHT: Afternoon shadows are cast on the grand concourse of Kansas City Union Station.

BELOW: The lobby of Union Station houses restaurants and gift shops.

OVERLEAF: Evening descends on downtown Kansas City and Union Station in this view from the hill of Liberty Memorial and the National World War I Museum.

Opened in 1914, Union Station became a crossroads for Kansas City and for travelers from across the nation. The gray limestone station built on a grand scale was one of the first large commissions for the young architect, Jarvis Hunt. Drawing from architectural ideas expressed in the Chicago World's Fair of 1893, Hunt incorporated themes from the Beaux-Arts and City Beautiful movements into his design of Union Station. Railroad baron, Edward Harriman, was said to advise Hunt to "Make a monument." When the 1920s rolled around, most Kansas City residents and rail passengers coming through Union Station thought that Hunt had succeeded.

Kansas City Union Station served the city and the traveling public well. Celebrities, politicians, writers, mobsters, and ordinary people passed through Kansas City Union Station. The war years of the 1940s took a toll on the station facilities. When World War II was over, the 1950s held great promise for railroads and rail travel as America enjoyed postwar prosperity. Streamliner trains came from the Santa Fe, Missouri Pacific, Union Pacific, Kansas City Southern, and Burlington. At the same time the automotive industry shifted into high gear. As road systems improved under President Dwight Eisenhower, more Americans took to their Chevrolets and Fords leaving the trains in their rear view mirrors.

By 1972, American railroads gave up the losing battle to save the passenger trains and turned their once busy services over to the federal government with the creation of Amtrak. Kansas City Union Station

ABOVE: A sculptural wreath encircles the exterior of one of the windows of Kansas City Union Station.

BELOW: The lobby of Kansas City Union Station leads to the concouse in this view from the second floor.

Above: Amtrak's Southwest Chief is at the Santa Fe Railroad Station in Newton, Kansas just west of Kansas City, Missouri in 1983. The southern and northern transcontinental lines of the Santa Fe join west of Newton.

Left: A circular window illuminates the second floor of Kansas City Union Station.

suffered too, and the once great lobby had the ignominious placement of a large plastic inflatable bubble inside to provide shelter for the few passengers still riding passenger trains on Amtrak.

Union Station was placed on the National Register of Historic places in 1972, but this designation did not stop the deterioration of Hunt's masterpiece. The roof leaked, the plaster was falling from the walls, and the station became a shadow of her former self.

In 1996, Missouri and Kansas counties of the Kansas City area passed a ballot initiative, a small bi-state sales tax, to restore Union Station. As plans for possible uses were explored, some in the Kansas City community wanted to just tear the station down and start over. Regional leaders with a sense of preservation prevailed and Union Station was saved from demolition.

Today the historic monument to Kansas City and transportation houses restaurants, offices, and a science museum. The station still has an area in the depot devoted to two daily Amtrak trains. It is possible once again to enter the lobby of Union Station and feel the grandeur of architecture from a period when people dreamed of beautiful cities and ten year old boys could have their eyes opened to the world.

LEFT: A motorcyclist paces Union Pacific No. 844 and a short eastbound train in central Nebraska along US Highway 30 on June 29, 2012. The steam train is returning from display at the College World Series in Omaha, NE.

RIGHT: Two sandhill cranes fly over the Union Pacific mainline along the Platte River in central Nebraska.

19 Union Pacific: A Nebraska Icon on the Overland Route

In 1862 America was at war with itself, and the outcome seemed undecided. In the midst of this great unknown, President Abraham Lincoln signed into existence the Pacific Railroad Act on July 1, 1862. Lincoln secured the unity of the nation and shaped the future of the country by authorizing the first transcontinental railroad. The Union Pacific Railroad was born as a result of that act. The transcontinental railroad started in Council Bluffs, Nebraska and connected with the Central Pacific coming from California. The two railroad met at Promontory Point, Utah on May 10, 1869. The Central Pacific later became the Western Pacific, but the Union Pacific has retained its corporate identity throughout this time.

It is doubtful that Lincoln could have imagined the UP of today. The Union Pacific is a giant of a railroad that serves the West and Midwest, hauling coal out of the Powder River Basin, moving corn and wheat to milling companies and bringing new automobiles to the the heartland.

The frequent appearance of vintage passenger trains across the Overland Route through the years has afforded railfans numerous chances to photograph recreations of UP passenger trains in historic locations. The UP maintains a fleet of steam locomotives in Cheyenne, Wyoming that boasts a 4-8-4 Northern type locomotive, No. 844, an engine that was built in 1941 and has never been out of service. An even larger steam locomotive, No. 3985, a restored 4-6-6-4, Challenger type engine, has delighted train lovers across the country with excursions over the past 20 years.

Now the UP is undertaking the renovation of one of its most famous and largest steam engines ever built, Big Boy type, No. 4014, a 4-8-8-4 wheel arrangement. The Big Boy was donated to the Southern California Chapter of the National Railway Historical Society in Pomona, California on December 7, 1961. The NRHS chapter transferred ownership of 4014 back to the UP in 2013 in anticipation of its return to steam.

The UP also maintains three E-9 diesel locomotives and with the steam engines comprise what the railroad calls its Heritage Fleet Operations. These iconic E-9 cab units sometimes provide power for the Armour Yellow,gray, and red passenger coaches in special trains that run over the line when the steam engines stay home. The diesels often serve as back-up to the steam locomotives selected excursions. The Heritage Fleet Operations locomotives are maintained at shop facilities in Cheyenne.

The Union Pacific Railroad is conscious of its image and the role the rail line has played in American history. In 2012, the UP celebrated the important milestone of 150 years under the same corporate name. A unique, interactive website called "UP 150" offered historical timelines, photographs, and video to the public. A contest challenging film makers to create a new version of a 1970s UP television commercial added to the festivities.

To the enjoyment of many, the railroad took its classic streamliner passenger trains around the system for local and national celebrations of UP railroading. No. 844 provided the power for these excursions with backup power from E-9 diesel locomotive, No. 949.

Below: Union Pacific No. 844 steams through central Nebraska on April 2, 2010.

Right: : UP No. 844 emerges from a blizzard east of Cheyenne, Wyoming pulling an early season eastbound train.

LEFT: UP diesel No. 949, an EMD E-9, provides backup power for steam engine No. 844 as a short westbound train passes through Gibbon, Nebraska on June 29, 2012.

ABOVE RIGHT: UP No. 844 and a short westbound train have spent the night in North Platte, NE. Crews prepare the train for departure.

OVERLEAF: UP No. 844 runs at track speed across the Nebraska mainline on April 2, 2010.

One of the unique UP excursions that has existed since 1908 is the annual Denver Post Cheyenne Frontier Days specials. In the early days of the Denver Post Special the train carried business and community leaders of Denver, Colorado to the annual Cheyenne Frontier Days Rodeo on the first Saturday of the rodeo each year. The rodeo is always the last week in July. The Denver Post Special did not run in 1942-1946 because of the rationing of supplies during World War II. In 1970 the special train was dropped by the railroad and the newspaper. Part of the reason for the cessation was that the train was so popular there were more Denver residents wrangling for invitations on the train than there were places available. The train was just too popular.

The train resumed to much fanfare in 1993. Today, the Special is more egalitarian and open to the paying public, but it is still so popular that a lottery system is used to distribute the 750 tickets available. Tickets are around $315 and give holders access to the Saturday afternoon rodeo and the the Cheyenne Fairgrounds where carnival rides and exhibits are situated.

LEFT: Steam engine crews inspect No. 844 in North Platte, NE on June 29, 2012.

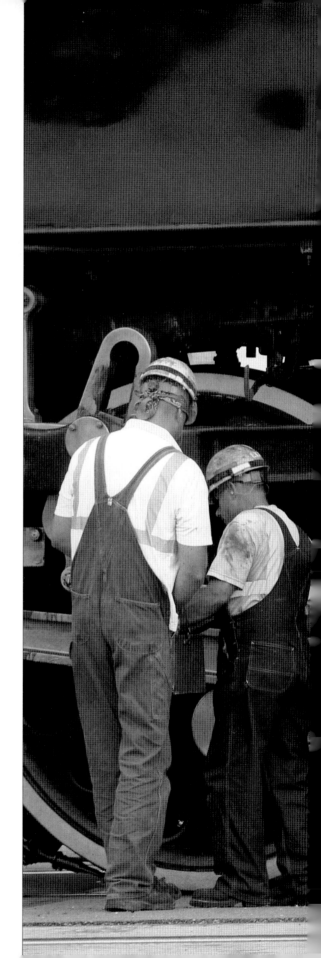

RIGHT: Crew service steam engine No. 844 at a brief stop in Fremont, NE on June 29, 2012.

The Denver Post Special is usually pulled by one of the UP's steam locomotives, but has also been powered by one of the vintage diesels in the Heritage Fleet Operations pool. Sometime the power for the special train is a mix of steam and diesel power.

During the last couple of years, the UP has sent its steam locomotive, No. 844 to Omaha, Nebraska for display during the annual College World Series of baseball. The steam engine sits across the street from the TD Ameritrade Park in the city.

In the past a steam special has sometimes departed Cheyenne eastbound across Nebraska on an early spring excursion during the month of March. The train's migration along the Platte River has then corresponded with one of the most unique bird migrations in the world. Close to 500,000 Sandhill Cranes can be found feeding in the stubble of harvested cornfields in Nebraska as the birds gather on an 80-mile section of river between Lexington and Grand island, Nebraska in what ornithologists call staging. For about four weeks in the late winter and early spring the birds rest and feast on the leftover corn in the fields. The birds fly to the gravel bars of the river at night for roosting. The cranes' migratory stopover is as amazing a sight as a Union Pacific locomotive steaming along the Platte River in frosty March weather. Sandhill Cranes and UP steam trains are part of the iconography of Nebraska and these windswept prairies.

Between Omaha and Cheyenne is North Platte, Nebraska, home to the world's largest railroad classification yard. The facility also has locomotive and repair shops and services some 750 diesel engines each month. The UP built a visitor center at the Bailey Yard that architecturally recalls the passenger depots along the railroad. An eight-story tower on the site, the Golden Spike Tower, allows visitors to watch the workings of the huge rail yard, the repair shops and the busy mainline. Inside the visitor center, guests can watch a movie about the railroad and view displays that tell the story of North Platte and the Union Pacific Railroad.

Little did Abraham Lincoln know in 1862 when he signed the Pacific Rail Act of 1862, that the Union Pacific would 150 years later still play such a vital role in America's commerce. Cheyenne's tag for their world famous Frontier Days rodeo each July is "The daddy of 'em all." The same title might apply to the railroad that founded Cheyenne. The Union Pacific is indeed "The daddy of em all" of American railroads, and steam still runs over the Overland Route in the 21st Century.

20 Cincinnati Union Terminal: An Art Deco Masterpiece

Like a giant Art Deco mantel clock, Cincinnati Union Terminal sits above I-75 and the Mill Creek Valley northwest of downtown Cincinnati, Ohio. This architectural masterpiece from 1933 is impressive whether seen in early morning light or at night when strategically placed floodlights illuminate this icon from the Great Depression. Water cascades in a series of falls into a pool at the foot of a fountain in front of the train station.

Cincinnati Union Terminal joins other railroad stations like Los Angeles Union Station, Philadelphia's 30th Street Station and Kansas City's Union Station in defining the city they serve. There is no other intact edifice quite like CUT.

A team of architects that included Alfred Fellheimer, Steward Wagner, Paul Phillippe Cret and Roland Wank designed the Terminal on the cusp of the economic collapse of the 1930s. The elegant half-dome of the station's front rises 108 feet into the air looking down over the cascading in front of the station.

Site preparation began in 1928 with massive amounts of fill dirt for the terminal's foundation. The station took five years to build and opened on March 31, 1933 with a final cost of $14.5 million dollars.

Architects Wank and Cret created space in the Terminal for a series of murals that would tell the story of the heritage of Cincinnati and the United States. Winold Reiss, a German immigrant, received the commission for this monumental mural project. Reiss is best remembered for his vibrant paintings of the Blackfeet Indians of Montana and his portraits of people from Harlem, New York. For his work in the Cincinnati train station, Reiss designed drawings of the murals to one-third scale. The Ravenna Tile Company in New York then cut glass mosaic tiles to create Reiss' vision in the rotunda and concourse of the station. Reiss produced 23 murals in the terminal that depicted the two timelines. Working from photographs, the German artist's murals featured Native Americans, early pioneers, engineers, and factory and construction workers.

LEFT: The neon sign showing the direction to trains is restored and in place in the lobby of Cincinnati Union Terminal.

RIGHT: Cincinnati Union Terminal glows at night behind the cascading fountain of this historic train station. Today CUT houses a museum and shopping complex.

A second artist, Pierre Bourdelle, produced paintings and wall carvings for the dining rooms, a hallway, restrooms, and a theater inside the Union Terminal. On the exterior facade of the CUT, sculptor Maxfield Keck, carved two bas relief murals depicting transportation and commerce. They frame the sides of the front of the station.

Cincinnati Union Terminal served eight major railroads during its early years in the 1930s and '40s. Those rail lines included the Baltimore and Ohio Railroad, the Chesapeake and Ohio Railroad, the Southern Railway, the Pennsylvania Railroad, the Louisville and Nashville Railroad, the Cleveland, Cincinnati, Chicago, and St. Louis Railway, and the Norfolk and Western Railway.

Passenger trains bearing exotic names served the new station. The N&W proudly ran the Powhatan Arrow, powered by their streamlined J-class steam locomotives that included No. 611. The Hummingbird and the Pan-American were Cincinnati trains of the L&N. The C&O had their own streamlined steam locomotives like No. 490 that powered the George Washington and the FFV, Fast Flying Virginian, into Cincinnati. Locomotive No. 490 is now preserved at the B&O Museum in Baltimore, Maryland. The N&W No. 611 is displayed at the Virginia Museum of Transportation in Roanoke, Virginia and could one day return to operation. Locomotives No. 611 and No. 490 are still remembered in Ohio. A wall mural in the downtown of nearby Columbus, Ohio depicts super life-size images of both steam engines.

OPPOSITE PAGE, TOP: The painted dome of Cincinnati Union Terminal forms a pleasing circular shape in this Art Deco train station from the1930s.

OPPOSITE PAGE, LOWER LEFT: The information desk in Cincinnati Union Terminal has classic Art Deco lines.

OPPOSITE PAGE, LOWER RIGHT: Norfolk and Western steam locomotive No. 611 ran an active excursion schedule through the 1980s into the early '90s. The engine sometimes pulled the N&W Powhatan Arrow to CUT.

BELOW: The lines of Cincinnati Union Terminal are quintessential Art Deco from the 1930s. The station is striking in early morning light.

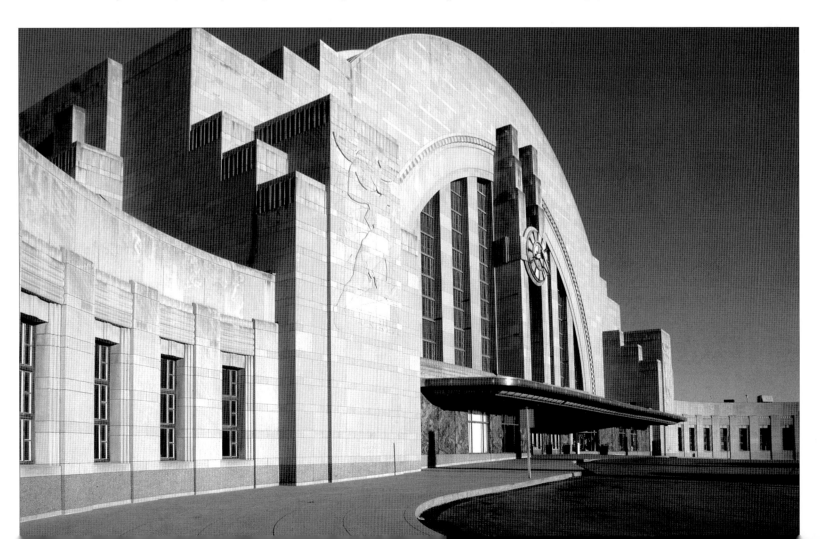

ABOVE: The classical Art Deco forms of Cincinnati Union Terminal in Cincinnati, Ohio are sharply illuminated in this early morning light.

LEFT: The Art Deco lines of Cincinnati Uion Terminal in Cincinnati, Ohio resemble a vintage mantel clock from the 1930s.

The station serviced more than 200 trains per day after its opening. World War II brought a large increase in traffic through the station. After the war, optimism about the future of passenger trains gave way to the lowered expectations of railroads as Americans fell in love with the automobile as a preferred way of travel. The nationalized passenger trains of Amtrak took over most passenger rail service in the U.S. in 1971. Ironically, in the same year that CUT was placed on the National Register of Historic Places, Amtrak abandoned Union Terminal and moved to a smaller facility in the downtown area along the Ohio River.

The city of Cincinnati purchased the station complex in 1975. For a time it appeared that the Joseph Skilken Organization might give new life to CUT with development of the facility as the "Land of Oz." This enterprise had a skating rink, bowling alley, restaurants, shopping malls, and other entertainment. By 1984, this attempt at a mall in CUT had failed and the station stood vacant for the next several years.

In 1985, the Museum of Natural History and the Cincinnati History Society chose CUT as its site for a new Museum Center. Four years later the Museum Center offered the Cincinnati Railroad Club the use of Tower A at the station. Tower A once housed the interlocking machines that controlled all train

RIGHT: : Early morning light spills over the gardens and classic Art Deco forms of Cincinnati Union Terminal.

BELOW: Norfolk and Western No. 611 often pulled the Powhatan Arrow from Norfolk, Virginia to Cincinnati, Ohio in the 1950s.

BELOW: Another locomotive that powered trains into CUT was Chesapeake and Ohio No. 490, now preserved at the B&O Railroad Museum.

movement through the Union Terminal complex. When originally built, Tower A had space for 231 operating levers. In 1990 the railroad club began restoration of the tower that sits on the back side of the station's dome. By 1991 the club completed the restoration and moved into their new space. Tower A has become a meeting place, museum, library, and gift shop. Admission is free. Each year the group sponsors a summer conclave of rail fans from around the country that gathers at CUT for a one day session of multi-media slide and AV presentations. In 1991 Amtrak returned to Cincinnati Union Terminal and provides service for the Cardinal, a passenger train that connects New York City, Cincinnati, and Chicago three times a week.

In 2014, the CUT Museum Center has an Omnimax Theater that screens the latest large format movies. The Center also houses the Cincinnati History Museum, the Duke Energy Children's Museum, the Museum of Natural History and Science, and the John A Ruthven Exhibition Gallery. The Museum Center also supports the Richard and Lucile Durrell Edge of Appalachia Preserve. This 16,000-acre tract of land on the border of the eastern mountains 75 miles from Cincinnati has educational and outdoor recreational opportunities for people of all ages.

21 The Lost Engines of Roanoke

They are called the Lost Engines of Roanoke. They might also be called the four steam locomotives that time forgot. Thanks to a group of railroad enthusiasts and the Virginia Museum of Transportation in Roanoke, Virginia, the locomotives that sat rusting in the Virginia Scrap Iron and Metal Company's rail yard in that city are now saved from the scrapper's torch.

When the four engines were sent to the junk yard in the 1950s, the Norfolk and Western Railroad was still building new steam locomotives. The group included No. 917, a 2-8-0, and three 4-8-0 steam engines, No. 1118, No. 1134 and No. 1151. Also in the group of Lost Engines of Roanoke were two Baldwin diesels N&W Nos. 662 and 663. There were also a couple of locomotive tenders, a flat car, and some hopper cars that were rescued from the scrap yard.

While photographing N&W No. 611 and No. 1218 at a special *Railfan* event at the Virginia Museum of Transportation in Roanoke, I walked down the road to the edge of the museum's rail yard and discovered No. 1151. This steam engine was built in the N&W Roanoke shops in 1911. The locomotive is a mastodon-type, the M2 classification, with four leading trucks, eight driving wheels, and no trailing trucks. Locomotives of this type were the primary type of power used by the N&W in the early years of the 20th century before the arrival of giant articulated freight-haulers like N&W No. 1218 that is also preserved at the museum.

After I returned home, I learned about these lost engines, by reading the website devoted to the locomotives. I called the executive director of the Virginia Museum of Transportation, Bev Fitzpatrick for more information.

As I talked with Fitzpatrick by telephone, he was jubilant because he had just announced to the press a a large donation from the Norfolk Southern Railway in the "Fire-Up 611" campaign. The N&W No. 611 is a streamlined 4-8-4 that is on display at the museum after an active life pulling excursions in the 1980s. The effort to return the locomotive to service is ongoing in 2014.

RIGHT: Norfolk and Western steam locomotive No. 1151 is one of the engines rescued from a Roanoke, VA scrap yard. This relic from the steam era is stored at the Virginia Museum of Transportation.

LEFT: Volunteers at the Virginia Museum of Transportation in Roanoke, Virginia prepare Norfolk and Western steam locomtoive No. 611 for a night photo session in July 2013. There is a possibility of renovation of this engine to active status in 2014.

RIGHT: A Norfolk Southern passenger coach sits in the yard of the Virginia Museum of Transportation in Roanoke, VA. Buildings of the city rise in the distance.

BELOW: Rusting parts of N&W No. 1151 await cosmetic restoration at the Virginia Transportation Museum in Roanoke, VA.

We talked about both No. 611 and the lost engines and were pleased that this J-class N&W locomotive had not joined No. 1151 and her sisters long ago. I also learned that the term, Lost Engines of Roanoke, probably came from a painting done by Fitzpatrick's brother, an artist, done in the 1980s.

Locomotive No. 1511 and her sister engine No. 1134 were among the oldest engines on the railroad when they arrived at the scrap yard on June 12, 1950. These locomotives might have remained forgotten or even worse broken down and sold for their valuable metal. Instead they sat rusting in the weeds at the scrap yard for over 50 years.

The discarded steam locomotives belonged to the Virginia Scrap Iron and Metal Company owned by Sam Golden. When Golden died in 2003, his estate gave all of the equipment to the Virginia Museum of Transportation in 2006, but the pieces had to be moved because a new commercial complex was planned for the site of the scrap yard.

In July 2008, the Western Virginia Preservation Society in Natural Bridge, Virginia, announced the beginning of a campaign to find new homes for the railroad equipment.

"We bartered and traded with a bunch of friends," said Fitzpatrick discussing the museum's role in trying to move all of this equipment. The VMT was especially interested in the No. 1151 because it was originally built in the N&W's Roanoke shops. The other three locomotives had been produced in Richmond, Virginia's N&W shops. On July 8, 2008, a Belleville, Ohio restaurant transported N&W No. 917 to the Buckeye State for display and use at the head end of a train used as a railroad theme restaurant. The locomotive was partially restored cosmetically. In 2009 the VMT moved No. 1151 to the museum's rail yard.

The other engines and equipment eventually found homes through the trading done by the VMT. No. 1134 was moved and restored for display at the new Railroad Museum of Virginia in Portsmouth, Virginia in 2010. Through trades with the Roanoke NRHS, No. 1118 was swapped for the No. 34, an 0-8-0T tank engine.

Fitzpatrick's history with Roanoke railroading and the Virginia Museum of Transportation is as remarkable as the fact that four sixty-year-old steam engines escaped their demolition in the 1950s. Fitzpatrick is a life-long resident of Roanoke, and he served on the Board of Directors of the museum at age 15 years. After college, Fitzpatrick became a banker with the Dominions Bank Shares Corporation where he was vice president for economic development and legal affairs until his retirement seven years ago at age 60. At retirement he became the executive director of the VMT.

Fitzpatrick has many dreams for the museum. One of the first is to see No. 611 restored and running. "We figure that the steam engine renovation will take about $500,000-$750,000," he said. The rest of the money of the goal of $3.1 million will go toward construction of a shop to maintain and store the legendary N&W locomotive.

RIGHT: Norfolk and Western locomotive No. 1151 is one the Lost Engines of Roanoke that was saved from demolition in a local scrap yard. The steam engine sits on the property of the Virginia Museum of Transportation and may one day be cosmetically restored for display at the museum.

Another goal for the museum said Fitzpatrick is the construction of a back shop exhibit area on the VMT's property where the museum's 1151 would be displayed with interactive features. Rather than a full cosmetic restoration, the locomotive would be sandblasted, moved inside the shop, and become suspended by two display cranes to resemble the shops where it was built in Roanoke in 1911.

With Bev Fitzpatrick's enthusiasm, all of those goals, including the resumption of steam excursion with N&W No. 611 seem possible.

"We have fun everyday. We don't make any money, but we have fun," he said as we finished our telephone conversation.

RIGHT: A side view of N&W No. 1151 shows the distinctive profile of this steam engine, a 2-8-0 type.

BELOW: A valve on N&W No. 1151 shows the varied patterns of oxidation on this steam engine saved from scrapping in Roanoke, VA at the Virginia Museum of Transportation.

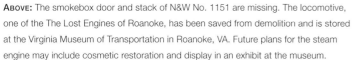
ABOVE: The smokebox door and stack of N&W No. 1151 are missing. The locomotive, one of the The Lost Engines of Roanoke, has been saved from demolition and is stored at the Virginia Museum of Transportation in Roanoke, VA. Future plans for the steam engine may include cosmetic restoration and display in an exhibit at the museum.

22 Grain Elevators: Prairie Skyscrapers

Crossing the Great Plains of North America can be a spiritual experience. A big sky above, immense distances ahead, and general emptiness is humbling. There is plenty of time to consider the nature of life on earth.

There is wheat, rolling like ocean waves, blowing in the wind to the horizon as you drive the prairies of Canada and the United States. Towns of the Great Plains revolve around agriculture and cattle, community and church, trucks and tractors, railroads and grain elevators. Food: for the body and soul.

The distances are great. From Kansas City to Denver is 645 miles. Minneapolis, Minnesota to Choteau, Montana on the Rocky Mountain Front is 1027 miles. Traveling these routes once took months by horse and wagon. Now the time required is one to two weeks by bicycle, two days of hard driving by car, one day by train, and two hours by airplane.

Grain elevators serve as marks on a giant ruler laid out on the Great Plains. Thrusting their towers a couple of hundred feet into the air, these elevators give a measure of time and distance for the traveler. For the general aviation pilot flying low and slow, gleaming white elevators can provide a good idea as to location since the name of the community is often painted on the sides in large readable letters.

These cathedrals of the plains, skyscrapers of the prairie, appear on the horizon on average every 10-12 miles apart and they usually denote the presence of a prairie town. That magic number of miles, 10-12, between prairie towns was determined during the late 1800s and early 20th century when railroad surveyors determined where their tracks would be planted. Citizens then decided where their towns might be built to have access to transportation. Ten miles was usually a day's wagon ride for the farmer bringing his crop to town. The needs of the steam engine also ordained the distance between towns. Locomotives needed water and service about every 10 or 12 miles. Prairie towns sprang up around these water stops. Grain collection facilities were then built. Some communities thrived. Others eventually dwindled.

LEFT: On the Rocky Mountain Front in northern Montana wheat pours out of a combine hopper into a truck trailer for transport to the local grain elevator in Choteau, MT.

RIGHT: Spokane, Portland, and Seattle steam locomotive No. 700 passes the Teslow grain elevator as she leaves Livington, MT on the morning of October 14, 2002.

After settlers on the prairies got fields tilled and a few crops under their belts, they moved beyond farming just for their family needs. Wheat and corn in abundance during those first fertile years gave surpluses that could be turned into cash. Grain elevators appeared as local community cooperatives to give farmers places to store their grain until shipment to market or until prices became higher.

Linda Laird in her book *The American Grain Elevator: Function and Form* groups the types of grain storage facilities on the Great Plains into the following classifications.

First there are line elevators that were built by companies that constructed a series of storage facilities from a single corporate location. These elevators often had the name of the company painted in large letters and logos on the sides of wooden and sheet metal clad structures. You can still see these "ghost signs" on the prairie surviving into the 21st Century.

Mill elevators developed as a way for milling companies to store enough grain to keep the processors in business through most of the year's production of flour and cereals, even when the harvest was finished by late summer. These mill storage facilities became quite large in capacity.

Farmers began building their own storage facilities as a way to hold their own grain without the added cost of paying another company. During the 1950s as railroad lines in wheat company were abandoned, some farmers took over line elevators left without rail service. One such elevator exists at the former community of Agawam on the former Milwaukee Railroad north of Choteau, Montana.

BELOW: The Teslow grain silo is part of the agricultural storage facility in Wilsall, Montana on July 9, 2012.

RIGHT: A Burlington Northern Santa Fe freight picks up speed along US Highway 2 east of Browning, Montana.

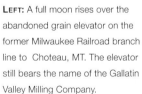

LEFT: A full moon rises over the abandoned grain elevator on the former Milwaukee Railroad branch line to Choteau, MT. The elevator still bears the name of the Gallatin Valley Milling Company.

OVERLEAF: Steam locomotive No. 844 pulls a short train westbound through a canyon of grain elevators in Chappell, NE on June 30, 2012.

In the early 20th century as American farmers increased their yields through the use of scientific methods applied to agriculture, farmers' cooperative elevators came into existence. This type of elevator still provides farmers of today an efficient way to store grain until the price or demand is at its best.

Grain facilities are called elevators because the wheat, barley or other grain is elevated by mechanical buckets from the collection pit where the grain has been dumped by trucks from the farm. Powered by motors from a head house at the top of the elevator, the grain is lifted skyward to be deposited into a series of long vertical bins for storage. Gravity is then employed when the grain is delivered to a rail car or tractor trailer truck for transport to a milling facility. The farmer bringing the grain to the elevator receives credit for the weight of his grain load, its moisture content, protein, and quality. The farmer may sell his grain to the elevator for a set price at the time of delivery or he may instruct the elevator operator to wait until prices reach a desired level.

ABOVE: Spokane, Portland, and Seattle No. 700 pulled an excursion train from Portland, Oregon to Spokane Washington in 2001. Here the rear observation coach glides past grain elevators in the wheat country of eastern Washington.

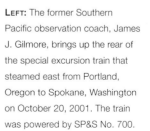

LEFT: The former Southern Pacific observation coach, James J. Gilmore, brings up the rear of the special excursion train that steamed east from Portland, Oregon to Spokane, Washington on October 20, 2001. The train was powered by SP&S No. 700.

LEFT: A vintage truck pulls a trailer over the Montana Rail Link tracks past the grain elevator at Reed Point, MT.

ABOVE: An abandoned dump truck sits in the grass below the grain elevators at Reed Point, MT. The elevators sit on tracks of the Montana Rail Link that runs along the Yellowstone River between Billings and Livingston, MT.

Grain elevators on the prairie were first built of wood. Early construction techniques after the Civil War involved simple stud construction with planed lumber. A later development and one still used on the northern plains is crib construction where boards are laid flat and spiked together. A common threat to wooden grain elevators during the steam train era was fire from sparks from passing locomotives. Sparks from motors combined with the dust inherent in elevator operations can also produce explosions and fires.

In the early 1900s many wooden elevators were covered with galvanized sheet metal. The Canadian provinces in wheat country are known for their surviving wooden elevators, many of which are painted red with logos of the company owning the facility emblazoned on the sides. These grain elevators provide stark vertical relief to the rolling horizontal seas of wheat and barley.

In the middle prairies of the U.S., concrete has proven to be a workable and efficient material for grain elevator construction. In cities like Wichita, Kansas the terminal elevators have grown to massive dimensions and can be seen on the horizon long before the city limits are approached when traveling by car.

Grain elevators and railroads are co-dependent. One may exist without the other, but the best way to transport wheat, corn or barley long distances is still by rail. The best place to store this "staff of life," is the grain elevator. They remain a poignant symbol of man's habitation of the epic Great Plains landscape.

23 Steamtown National Historic Site and the Tunkhannock Viaduct

Descending by car into the valley of Nicholson, Pennsylvania brings a surprise to many first-time visitors. Coming from Scranton, Pennsylvania on state HW 11, the former Delaware, Lackawanna, and Western Railroad tracks, now Canadian Pacific, run parallel to the highway on a hill above the roadway. Suddenly the road bends around a curve and dives into valley of the Tunkhannock River. The railroad continues on across the valley on the Tunkhannock Viaduct. The viaduct gracefully spans the valley and the village of Nicholson in the heart of the Pocono Mountains. The concrete arch trestle is 2,375 feet in length

The Tunkhannock Viaduct, also called the Nicholson Bridge, is about 30 miles from downtown Scranton. The trestle is constructed of reinforced concrete and is still the largest such concrete bridge in the world. The dazzling white bridge spans mountains on either side of Nicholson at 240 feet above the river and the village. The trestle came into being as part of a relocation of the Lackawanna Railroad between Scranton and Binghamton, New York.

Construction on the trestle began on May 1912 and continued for two years. The bridge is composed of ten towering arches measuring 180 feet apart. There are smaller arches above each of the ten large arches. Some 1,140 tons of steel and 167,000 cubic yards of concrete were used in the trestles construction. Soon after it was built, many considered the Tunkhannock Viaduct one of the great wonders of the world.

While driving in Nicholson, it is difficult not to look up toward the towering, gleaming trestle at frequent intervals. I am sure if you lived in the town you would become used to the sight of such an impressive structure, but for the visitor, the viaduct is hard to ignore. It is like staying at the El Tovar Hotel on the south rim of the Grand Canyon and trying not to look out to the yawning chasm every few minutes.

Surprisingly, what you see above the valley is only part of the story. Like an iceberg in the North Atlantic, much of the Tunkhannock Viaduct lies beneath the surface. Burton Cohen designed the bridge and G. J. Ray was the chief engineer. The crews worked between 1913 and 1914 drilling down through the valley floor to bedrock 130 feet to sink some of the concrete piers.

LEFT: The former railroad station for the Delaware, Lackawanna and Western Railroad in Scranton, PA is now a Radisson Hotel.

RIGHT: The Nicholson Viaduct, also known as the Tunkhannock Viaduct, rises high above the valley floor and the village of Nicholson, PA.

The Tunkhannock Viaduct is not the only reinforced concrete bridge with graceful open arches on the old Lackawanna railroad. Before the span at Nicholson, there was the Martins Creek Viaduct that had room for three tracks across the bridge. The Tunkhannock has only two sets of tracks. There are smaller but still impressive arched spans on parts of the abandoned Lackawanna line. Near Hainesburg, New Jersey, there is the Paulinskill Viaduct and over the Delaware River in Pennsylvania is the Slateford Junction bridge.

Because of the type of coal used by its steam locomotives and hauled by its trains, the Lackawanna was called the Road of Anthracite with Scranton, Pennsylvania lying at the center of the railroad connecting New York City and Buffalo, New York. Scranton is in the heart of coal country in Pennsylvania.

Today Scranton boasts one of only a few U.S. National Park units dedicated to preserving and telling the story of American railroading. The Steamtown National Historic Site is situated in the former rail yards of the old Lackawanna. A large part of the historic site is dedicated to preserving and running the

ABOVE: The logo for the Lackawanna Railroad was placed in the central arch of the railroad viaduct above Nicholson, PA.

RIGHT: Canadian National steam locomotive 3254 sits in the roundhouse of the Steamtown National Historic Site roundhouse in Scranton, PA.

OVERLEAF: The Tunkhannock Viaduct spans the valley of Tunkhannock Creek and the village of Nicholson, PA. The concrete bridge is 2,375 feet long and 240 feet above the valley floor.

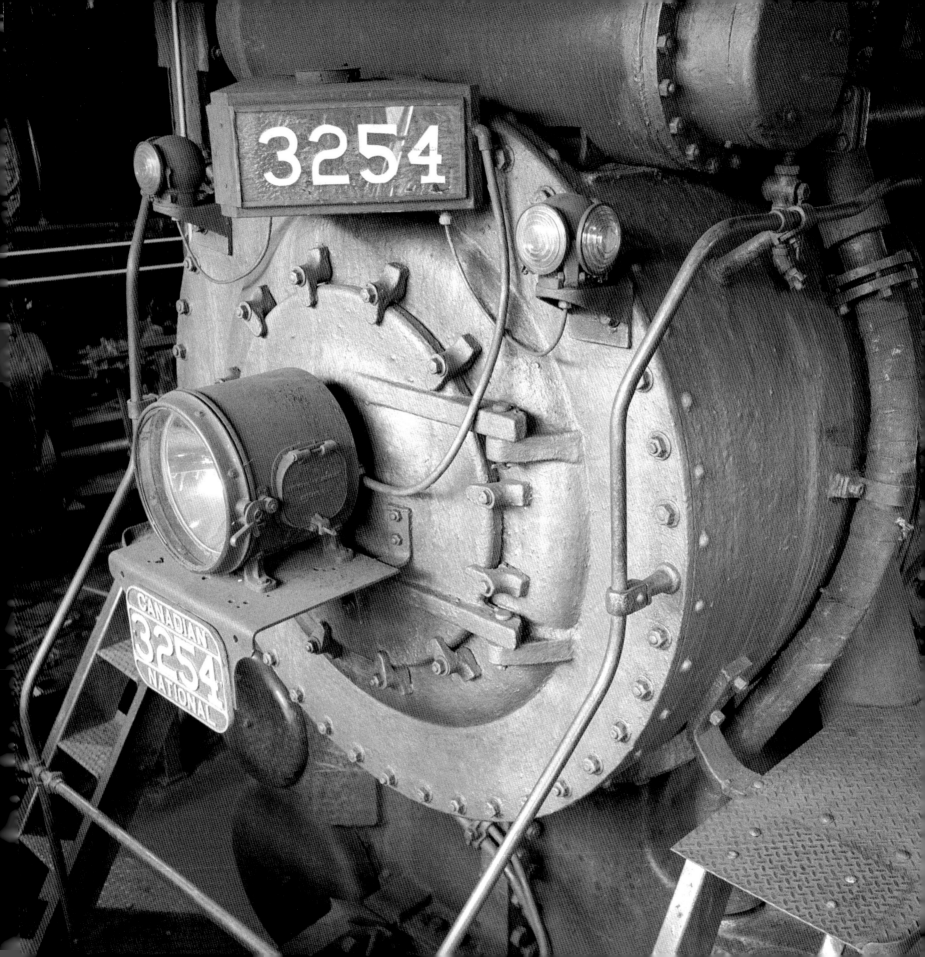

locomotives and rail cars assembled by New England business man, Nelson Blount. Most of the collection was maintained at Steamtown USA in Bellows Falls, Vermont. With Blount's death in 1967, financial support for the museum dwindled. The museum moved to Scranton in 1995 after Congress established Steamtown National Historic Site in 1986.

Steamtown has an active roundhouse and locomotive shop. There is an operating turntable on site and a number of preserved and operable diesel and steam locomotives. Excursion passenger trains operate in Scranton and sometimes on longer trips out of town. Tours and excursions around the Scranton yard demonstrate to visitors the function and activity of railroads during the height of the steam age.

Immediately adjacent to Steamtown NHS is a shopping mall with food courts and a variety of specialty and department stores. It is not at every mall that you can look out a window and see smoke and steam from a locomotive working in the Steamtown Yard. Visitors to Steamtown and Scranton can also stay at the former Lackawanna Station Hotel. This neoclassical style six-story hotel is on the National Register of Historic places. It is easy to imagine that as you settle in to bed, you have just crossed the Tunkhannock Viaduct as you came into town from Buffalo.

The National Historic Site also fulfills its mission of education by hosting RailCamp, a cooperative venture between the National Park Service and the National Railway Historic Society, for high school students. At camp, young people learn the details of maintaining and operating preserved, historic railroad locomotives, cars, and facilities. Students are housed in dorms of the University of Maryland in Wilmington, Delaware. Campers work both in Scranton at Steamtown and at the Strasburg Railroad and the Railroad Museum of Pennsylvania in Lancaster County, Pennsylvania.

With the passing of those who repaired and ran steam locomotives in the 1930s and '40s, a new generation today must learn these skills if our railroad heritage is to be preserved. Steamtown National Historic Site and NRHS is doing their part to pass on this knowledge with RailCamp. A visit to Steamtown, Scranton, and the the Tunkhannock Viaduct reminds us of the industrial greatness that was America in the 20th Century.

ABOVE: A young bicyclist pedals past tidy white frame homes that are situated under the Tunkhannock Viaduct in Nicholson, PA.

RIGHT: A truck turns onto Pennsylvania State Highway 92 under the spans of the Tunkhannock Viaduct rise 240 feet above the village of Nicholson, PA.

RIGHT: Pennsylvania State Highway 92 passes under one of the high concrete arches of the Tunkhannock Viaduct in Nicholson, PA.

Acknowledgments

This book was produced with much help along the way. I thank Colin Gower who made this publication possible. Thanks go to designer, Phil Clucas, who did the layout and patiently awaited my next slug of images and text jamming his email inbox.

I had tremendous help from Lynn Wasson who was always willing to look at one more chapter. Pam Pearce gave needed advice in helping organize and rearrange my text in several chapters . Ted Benson, one of my heroes of railroad photography, looked at photographs and read a section of my manuscript. Thanks, Ted, for reminding me of the difference between a grain elevator and a grain silo and that the Milwaukee Road used motors not electric locomotives in their Montana territory. Richard Grigsby, owner of the Reader Railroad, is a longtime friend, and I thank him for including me in his steam crews when making movies. Brenda Rouse, passenger agent, for the Arkansas and Missouri Railroad, was always ready to give me information and assistance on this jewel of an Ozark shortline.

Bev Fitzpatrick, executive director of the Virginia Museum of Transportation, told me the story of the Lost Engines of Roanoke. Gary Koehn at the Grapevine Vintage Railroad helped me understand some of the history of that excursion operation. Sandra Olson, director of the Waynoka Historical Society, was always happy to show me the progress of the Waynoka Air-Rail Museum and provide history of the Transcontinental Air Transport and the Santa Fe Railroad in Waynoka, Oklahoma. David Bell, my brother and mentor in photography was always willing to listen to one more idea for a chapter in this book. Thanks to Les Arensmeyer and Linda Laird who educated me about grain elevators.

Thanks to you all for helping me create this book of images and stories.

And last, thanks go to my wife, Candy Anderson Bell, who never complained on our travels across the country when she let me follow my nose and find that depot or roundhouse that I just knew was around the corner. Without her presence in my life, any creative urge would be lost.